THE HISTORY OF MIAMI HIP HOP

THE **STORY** OF **DJ KHALED, PITBULL, DJ CRAZE,** AND **OTHER CONTRIBUTORS** TO **SOUTH'S FLORIDA'S SCENE**

D1120643

JOHN CORDERO

MICROCOSM PUBLISHING
PORTLAND, ORE AND CLEVELAND, OHIO

HISTORY OF MIAMI HIP HOP
THE STORY OF DJ KHALED, PITBULL, DJ CRAZE, AND OTHER CONTRIBUTORS TO SOUTH'S FLORIDA'S SCENE

© 2022 John Cordero
© This edition Microcosm Publishing 2022
First edition - 3,000 copies - December, 2022
ISBN 978-1-62106-395-7
This is Microcosm #409
Cover by Lindsey Cleworth
Edited by Sarah Koch
Photos and illustrations by John Cordero unless otherwise labeled
Interior design by Gigi Little

To join the ranks of high-class stores that feature Microcosm titles, talk to your local rep: In the U.S. **COMO** (Atlantic), **ABRAHAM** (Midwest), **BOOK TRAVELERS WEST** (Pacific), **TURNAROUND** (Europe), **UTP/MANDA** (Canada), **NEW SOUTH** (Australia/New Zealand), **GPS** in Asia, Africa, India, South America, and other countries, or **FAIRE** in the gift trade.

For a catalog, write or visit:
Microcosm Publishing
2752 N Williams Ave.
Portland, OR 97227
https://microcosm.pub/Miami

LIBRARY OF CONGRESS CATALOGING-IN-PUBLICATION DATA

Names: Cordero, John, 1977- author.
Title: The history of Miami hip hop : the story of DJ Khaled, Pitbull, DJ Craze, and other contributors to South Florida's scene / by John Cordero.
Description: Portland : Microcosm Publishing, 2022. | Summary: "In the late 90s, the music scene in Miami was at the infancy of becoming the multi-million dollar cultural and artistic force that it is today. Musicians like Pitbull, DJ Khaled, and countless others staked Miami's claim as the newest Mecca for Hip Hop heads and graffiti artists. During this time, The Cipher was created. An independent newspaper that followed the scene and included reviews, interviews, essays, photos, and more, The Cipher was the choice source for discovering Miami's underground. The History of Miami Hip Hop chronicles the ups and downs of this legendary rag during its short tenure. Author John Cordero presents both a memoir of his time as one of the newspaper's creators, and an anthology of some of The Cipher's greatest hits. Both a love letter to The Cipher as well as 1990s Miami, this narrative is an essential chapter in the history of Hip Hop's third coast"-- Provided by publisher.
Identifiers: LCCN 2022020299 | ISBN 9781621063957 (trade paperback)
Subjects: LCSH: Rap (Music)--Florida--Miami--History and criticism. | Hip-hop--Florida--Miami. | Rap musicians--Florida--Miami.
Classification: LCC ML3531 .C665 2022 | DDC 782.421649759/381--dc23/eng/20220427
LC record available at https://lccn.loc.gov/2022020299

MICROCOSM · PUBLISHING

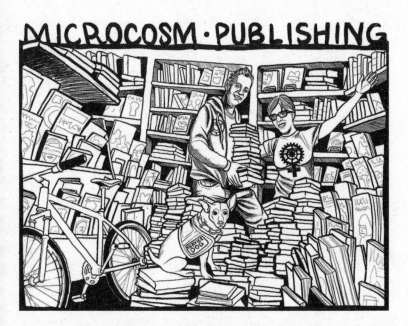

MICROCOSM PUBLISHING is Portland's most diversified publishing house and distributor with a focus on the colorful, authentic, and empowering. Our books and zines have put your power in your hands since 1996, equipping readers to make positive changes in their lives and in the world around them. Microcosm emphasizes skill-building, showing hidden histories, and fostering creativity through challenging conventional publishing wisdom with books and bookettes about DIY skills, food, bicycling, gender, self-care, and social justice. What was once a distro and record label was started by Joe Biel in a bedroom and has become among the oldest independent publishing houses in Portland, OR. We are a politically moderate, centrist publisher in a world that has inched to the right for the past 80 years.

Global labor conditions are bad, and our roots in industrial Cleveland in the 70s and 80s made us appreciate the need to treat workers right. Therefore, our books are MADE IN THE USA.

BAYFRONT BASH '98

ALL ACCESS

08.14..

CDUCTIVE

INDEPENDENT MUSIC & FILM
CONFERENCE
SEPTEMBER 28TH, 29TH, & 30TH

P A N E L I S T

steady building

PRESS

★ in the **PARK**

**Speedy Legs
Zulu Gremlin**
B-Boy event of the millenium

MEDIA

miami HIP HOP fest '98

VIP

Miami
ENTERTAINMENT
CONFERENCE '99

July 30-31
Wyndham Hotel,
Downtown Miami, Florida

Calling All Current and Future Stars!

Do you have the right stuff?

ALL ACCESS

B BOY MASTERS
PRO - AM
1999
May 20-23

Miami, FL

How Can I Be Down

1999
6

PETER THOM

presented by:

Teen RAGAZINE

SWAT
fest
99

FEATURING:

Everlast & Eve

ALSO PERFORMING:
Sumack, L.A.B & Ragazzi

ALL ACCESS

THE GRAFFBBQ
miami.florida.us
HOSTED BY
sponsored

Gigi Little

the CiPHeR

MiaMi's HiP HoP NeWSPaPeR

MIAMI'S HIP HOP NEWSP

ZULU N

DJ KHALED

ERYKAH BADU

The soul shining sister

Q-BERT

Invisible Scratch Pikl

Black Moe?

...united and it feels so good

CONTENTS

INTRODUCTION

When it comes to hip hop in Miami, just like the immigrants and transplants that have built the city, the scene has reinvented itself countless times. Shakin' what your mama gave ya and dancin' all night gave way to everyday I'm hustlin' and the trap. However, underneath the fast beats and glossy videos, there was a movement that maintained and expressed all aspects of the culture: walls and expressway signs drenched in graffiti, pirate and college radio stations pumpin' late night fat beats and rhymes, tiny hole-in-the-wall clubs giving shine to DJs spinning vinyl grooves, and a healthy mixtape scene promoted by flea markets and Hip Hop shops. It was into what is now considered the old Miami that my family and I arrived in the mid-90s.

I was already a fiend before I became a teen, deep, really deep, into hip hop: Graffiti, mixtapes, albums, vinyl, shows, *The Source*, *Rap Pages*, *Rap Sheet*, *Rap City*, rap, rap, rap. . . and I faithfully recorded a college radio station mix show every week from WPRK 91.5 FM at Rollins College, a liberal arts school in Orlando, featuring mixes by a guy you might have heard of: DJ Khaled.

Landing in a standard issue apartment complex in what locals call *La Souwesera* (Southwest Miami), I found myself with no crew and no backup. Kids around my way were not hip hop heads. They were more into Bone Thugs, Coolio, and whatever pop radio station Power 96 played. I liked the thuggish ruggish sound just like everybody else, but didn't care for a gangsta's paradise. Instead, heaven was on the left side of the radio dial. Within days of arriving, I had already found the University of Miami's WVUM 90.5 FM and community supported WDNA 88.9 FM, the two stations that played uncut hip hop.

This new environment gave me a gift that, at the time, completely blew my mind: the now defunct Malibu penit (now the Royal Palms apartment complex). An abandoned housing development at the intersection of the Dolphin and Palmetto expressways, it was filled with walls after walls of unbelievable, incredible masterpieces painted by the kings of Miami graf at the time: DAM, BSK, MSG, Inkheads, and others. These guys and gals had transformed an empty, derelict lot into an open-air museum. What split my wig was the fact that I lived just five blocks away! In no time at all, I was completely addicted and could be found there all day, every day.

According to miamigraffiti.com, the word "penit" is unique to South Florida: "The term has come to be used for any illegal graffiti oriented building (or buildings) that has become frequented by a variety of writers, or become an epicenter for graffiti in an area." And, of course, its roots weren't that far from me: "The original 'penit' was the graffiti warehouse located in the Fontainebleau area in South Doral. It was theorized that the building was intended to be a penitentiary but was never completed, so it was referred to as 'The Penit.'" And what do you know? I lived right down the street from one.

Content to tag and bomb, I knew I had nowhere near the skills required to put up a piece. So what? Hanging out there, I started meeting other writers from places like Kendall, Miami Lakes, Westchester, Hialeah, and Cutler Ridge who would drive up, park, and pull out crates of spray paint from their trunks. I stood amazed. It seemed like a summer camping trip! Some even brought girls (is spray paint an aphrodisiac?), boomboxes, and blunts. They would paint, smoke out, blast hip hop, take their flicks, and leave. Meanwhile, I'd walk home with my hands smeared with paint, bookbag falling apart with cans, and pockets full of spray tips.

Clearly this was the best summer ever, but it was coming to an end. I was 18 now, and the stakes were high. An arrest would mean county jail, meaning I had to be a little extra careful. With the fall semester looming, I enrolled at Miami-Dade Community College, seeking an A.A. in journalism. My dream was to write for *The Source*, *Rap Pages*, and all the other hip hop magazines I was devouring every month.

While the industry partied on South Beach at the "How Can I Be Down?" convention put on by Jimmy Henchmen and Peter Thomas, heads were at Roberto Clemente Park in Wynwood (pre-gentrification, no one wanted any part of that neighborhood back then). Focusing on blackbooks instead of textbooks, I attended my first Hoodstock because I was already down.

On that sunny day in October 1995, I took the 11 bus on 87th and Flagler to downtown, and then the 2 up Northwest Second Avenue to the park. As I arrived, mad heads were rolling up with blunts, blackbooks, and headphones. At first everyone just milled around as Rage and Ease from the Inkheads completed a piece on the handball court. Soon enough, as the park got full, the Boot Camp Clik rolled up in a promo van. Headz were ready, but I was front and center with Smif & Wessun, starting a convo with Steele and next thing you know, he's tagging my blackbook and telling me how he used to write while the Decepticons were getting busy in the BK in the late 80's. To round out the day, Fat Joe performed, along with Mad Lion, Channel Live, Akinyele, and the BCC. Little did I know that Hoodstock founder and promoter DJ Raw had a side gig moving weight, but at least he was doing something positive with his funds.

At the same time, I was already familiar with Wynwood before the walls went up due to going on solo expeditions looking for record stores to dig in. Before the art walks, the galleries, the murals, the hipsters, and the food trucks, this was a run-down depressed inner city ghetto. I noticed that aside from Zulu meetings and Hoodstock, few hip hop heads would come here, and what for? I'm not going to front like I was some fearless pioneer—truthfully, I had no idea that I wasn't supposed to go there! I was looking up record stores in the yellow pages, driving all over town to dig in the crates: Blue Note, Uncle Sam's, Raw Records and Tapes, and other long gone, defunct vinyl spots in Liberty City, Opa-Locka, and Hialeah. This was my Miami, my hip hop, my life. And it was time to document it all.

Hip Hop Queens crew getting down—Miami 1995

Working hard or hardly working at Spec's Music in South Beach (RIP)

Kickin' it with the Hip Hop Queens at Southwest High School—Miami 1995

Hip Hop Queens crew representing—Miami 1995

Dinner break from hosting duties on Miami-Dade College's radio station WKCR 1600 AM

With the homies Tino and Shareef kickin' it at MDCC's radio station

THE GOLDEN AGE

As 1995 progressed, I was schooling the younger heads at my complex on blunt smoking and graffiti writing. After meeting and becoming friends with a member of the Universal Zulu Nation at MDCC, I began regularly attending meetings in Wynwood. The Miami Chapter had been founded in 1993, and in two years, membership had expanded via show promotion and radio shoutouts. I had heard the Zulu references on records by A Tribe Called Quest and the Jungle Brothers before, so my interest was piqued by the fact that dope artists were affiliated with it.

As '95 (Year of the Wu-Tang) morphed into '96 (Year of the Outkast), hip hop was in its Golden Age, and so was Miami. The national hip hop media ignored us except to poke fun at Miami Bass and at the 2 Live Crew. Although some of my fellow heads dismissed the bass sound as booty shit, I was into it since the days of the Poison Clan, DJ Laz, and The Bass That Ate Miami (the documentary of the same name is highly recommended).

But contrary to popular belief that all we did was rap over "Planet Rock" all day, the New York influence was deep in South Florida as more and more heads were moving down from the 5 Boroughs, just as I had done from Orlando where there was a large Nuyorican population as well. With Miami being one of the most racially segregated cities in America, the sounds that dominated certain neighborhoods reflected their ethnic makeup. The majority Black American, Haitian, Bahamian, and Jamaican Northwest and Northeast sides were partial to bass, dance-hall, and hood rap, while heads in La Souwesera (the majority Hispanic Southwest) were either into the East Coast boom bap or the commercial crap on MTV and pop radio station Power 96.

Meanwhile, DJ Craze was just beginning his domination of the turntable world, graffiti crews were covering every available space all over the city, B-Boy battles were the norm at South Beach and other spots, and local MCs were battling and recording at Drunk Drew's Science Room and putting out vinyl, which got play on the two radio shows every self-respecting head taped each week: WVUM's *Hip Hop Shop* hosted by Darnella Dunham, and WDNA's *Saturday Night Funk Box* helmed by Arturo "Rhythm Rocker" Gomez with DJ Dundee on the decks.

The Shop broadcast from Coral Gables on Thursday nights at 10 p.m., and I was always ready with my tape pressing record. Its only drawback was that it was the University of Miami's radio station, so they played clean versions since it came on before midnight, which is when the FCC's safe harbor rules allowed dirty versions to play. Fortunately, the *Saaaaaaturday Night Funk Box* rhythm rocked from 1 to 4 a.m. on Saturdays from its studio on Coral Way as I would fall asleep to the hip hop lullabies.

It was on these two shows that I first heard The Laststrawze, Doz Funky Bastardz, Mother Superia, B-Dope, Da Alliance, NME, and other local rhymesayers. Mother Superia, from the Goulds area down south, had already independently released "The Rokk

Bottom," one of the first Miami Hip Hop anthems in 1993, which was produced by DJ Taz from DFB. Society's "Yes N Deed" (produced by DJ Slice and signed to Luke Records) came out in '94. Although most stayed local, Superia did sign a deal with 4th & B'Way. Unfortunately, her album, "Levitation," which had a 1996 release date and featured production by Reggie Noble and Kris Parker, was shelved and she was lost in the industry mix.

Another memorable release from this era was Da Alliance's "Fake Outta Towners" which called out all the herbs who fronted like they were "New Yorken" (not a typo, that's what we called them). The night I heard it on the *Hip Hop Shop*, I knew it would create a shitstorm. Hit dogs will holler, as the saying goes. They got clowned, called out as frauds, wack, you name it. But the crew they repped, Crazy Hood Productions, has always screamed Kendall. (Kendall is about as far from "hood" as you can get in Miami, and I respected them for that).

I found myself supporting their crusade full-on, because I too had seen some flaugin' ass clowns wearing Timbs and bubble vests in tropical 90-degree heat and humidity. The worst were the ones whose parents moved down to Miami from NYC back in the day, yet acted like they were thugs from the projects rather than from the nice part of Queens. I blasted Mobb Deep as much as the next guy, but I never felt the urge to wear Hennessy shirts or speak the Dunn language. To me, it was completely normal to listen to the latest Tony Touch mixtape and then Spanish radio station El Zol 95 right after. In one day, I could go to the Malibu penit to paint and

Akinyele performing at '95 Hoodstock

B-Girls on the set

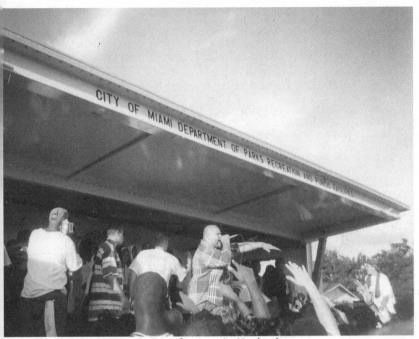

Fat Joe performing at '95 Hoodstock

Boot Camp Clik performing at '95 Hoodstock

then to the Dominican Independence Day festival at Bayfront Park downtown to jam to Ramon Orlando and "El Venado."

But even the fake outta towners knew that there was one spot that was hallowed ground for all: The Gates. This was a hip hop weekly put on at a hole-in-the-wall dive bar on Española Way in the beach (nowadays it's the Lost Weekend bar). Every Thursday night, DJ Craze summoned all heads from far and wide to worship at the altar of the boom bap. Before spots went 21+ and corporate, before the supermodel photoshoots, before any other club even played hip hop, and before all the industry conventions and videos turned it into a VIP playground, South Beach was actually kind of grimy although its "ghetto by the beach" rep was slowly fading away from its Cocaine Cowboys heyday (gentrification strikes again!).

Just down the block from The Gates, Washington Avenue was a popular cruise spot for cars driving by with the boomin system, while weed and coke were openly sold on the sidewalk, and most clubs were small and exclusive. But the Humble Lion promotion team went to work and in a blink of an eye The Gates was packed to full capacity. I saw plenty of heads get turned away due to either not having the right connection at the door, being clueless tourists, or trying to pose as hard rocks. Being introduced to the nightlife at The Gates taught me my first rap industry lesson: politics and connections open doors.

Because the Shaka Zulus were providing security, I was able to slide in on the humble, give dap, and just zone out all night. Their motto: "come in peace, or leave in pieces" couldn't have been more apt. There were many records and skulls broken in there. One night

Members of the Universal Zulu Nation—Miami Chapter

Getting up at the Malibu Penit—1995

when Craze premiered GZA's "Liquid Swords" promo single, after he played the first verse multiple fights broke out. Next thing I know Shaka Zulus were stomping heads, throwing dudes out the club . . .total chaos, mass confusion! With no choice but to stop playing the record, Craze got on the mic (a shocker, 'cause he never talked), telling people to calm the fuck down. Meanwhile to avoid the fists flying on the floor, I was on top of a speaker just losing my mind yelling. It was pure madness and I loved that shit! After order was restored, Craze backspun and played it back to back three times, since the whole club was screaming for it.

We locals take this for granted, but the only three places where you can party all night in the U.S.A. are NYC, Vegas, and Miami. Everyone else pretty much shuts down at 2 or 3 a.m. The Gates stayed open until 5, and it would be around 7 when I would get home. Breaking night became a ritual, a habit. Basically, my daily ritual was: draw in class, wear batteries out of my Walkman with Tony Touch and Craze mixtapes, visit my girlfriend, try to do homework, build with heads at Zulu meetings, and read whatever hip hop mag was around.

Now, I realize that most heads were strictly into the beats and rhymes, or the club scene, or the girls, the blunts, social activism, whatever. I was into all of that too, but it was nothing for me to read *120 Lessons*, *On The Go* magazine, and my class textbook all in one sitting. The Internet was in its infancy, relegated to complete nerd status and only available at school, but I was on it searching for the meaning of "Chill God, yo the sun don't chill Allah / what's todays' mathematics son? Knowledge God." Lyrics such as these were unknown to the 85, and even though I wasn't about to join the Nation of Gods and Earths, most commonly known as the 5 Percenters, I still had the hunger for more.

A couple of years before I arrived in town, a couple of heads organized the loose Miami Hip Hop community around a common cause. Omar Islam and Mentor, who then passed on the leadership to Erick X, established the Universal Zulu Nation-Miami chapter in 1993. Since its founding in the Bronx by Afrika Bambaatta in the mid-70's, the UZN had become a global organization with chapters as far away as Japan. Holding its meetings in Wynwood, it quickly became a hub of creativity, knowledge, and hip hop culture. Heads such as Mushroom, Brother Mike, Isaam, Chillski, Erick X, Simone, and Lady Diget were at the forefront of educating and schooling a generation of kids hungry for knowledge. A sample of suggested reading included "The New World Order," "Behold a Pale Horse," "The Meaning of Masonry," "The Trilateral Commission," and "The Isis Papers." Years before e-Tolls and iPhones, I already knew about microchips, the cashless society, and GPS trackers.

Of course, I formally joined the Zulu Nation after having memorized the 15 beliefs and taken them to heart: "We believe in truth wherever it may be found...we believe in the one god who is called by many names...we believe that through tricknology many are fooled..." on and on, faithfully attending every Thursday evening for my instruction, followed by a night of worship at the hip hop altar known as The Gates, and devouring all manner of books. It became my religion, even though "religion," the word, had a negative connotation as far as I was concerned: deaf, dumb, and blind sheeple worshipping a white Jesus. I was above it all with my 5 Percenter, I Self Lord And Master, Zulu Nation, enlightened, Eastern philosophy schtick. I loved the diversity and uncompromising stance of the Zulus' advocacy for hip hop culture as a positive force along with the emphasis on researching and not taking anything at face value. At eighteen years old, I would skip school with my girlfriend and instead of going to the beach or getting high, we went to the downtown main library and spent the day in the stacks!

Turned out that chapter leader Erick X lived not that far from me, on Southwest 87th Avenue and 8th Street near Coral Park High. Right around the corner was The Checkpoint, a hip hop store stocked with graf tips, t-shirts, and magazines. Every time I went, I scanned the literature hoping to find any type of coverage on our scene. No matter what, from glossy to b&w, there was nothing. For the time being, the seeds were being planted for an endeavor that would change the game, as industry heads would say.

From its one-sheet newsletter beginnings in a Harvard dorm room in the late 80s, *The Source* had grown to become the number one hip hop magazine in terms of circulation and rep. Although its masthead proclaimed it to be about "Hip Hop Music, Culture, and Politics," Miami just wasn't on their radar. Its competitors weren't any better. There was a complete lack of coverage in the hip hop press—it was as if we didn't exist. New York had *The Source*, *Vibe* (a Quincy Jones investment vehicle), *Ego Trip*, and *Stress*. Los Angeles held it down with *Rap Pages*, *Rap Sheet*, and *Urb*. The Bay Area had *4080*. However, Miami had nothing. When I was new in town, I had caught a copy of a b&w stapled issue of *FreeGround* at a record spot

Big Pun (L) and Fat Joe (R) performing at The Temple—1998

Marlon Pacheco

in Hialeah. To my knowledge, this was the only hip hop publication that was from Miami about Miami. The issue I picked up featured Mother Superia on the cover and contained interviews with KRS-One and the Rhythm Rocker. It was well put together and I fiended for another issue, but I never saw one again. As these were the pre-online days, it vanished.

Aside from the token disses at booty shaking and an occasional feature on Uncle Luke, Miami was M.I.A. from the rags and video shows. *The Source* did dedicate an entire issue to Miami Bass in 1995, but wasted five pages on Vanilla Ice. (Really? He's not even from Miami). At least our hometown newspaper, *The Miami Herald*, had half a clue: "South Florida's burgeoning hip-hop community has many homes," they wrote in 1995. "Pirate radio, garage DJs, even Universal SharpShooters warehouse, the North Miami Beach photography studio that doubles as a hip-hop hangout. But to many of South Florida's deffest rappers, The Science Room is the living room. It's a clubhouse and training ground." Mother Superia was a regular, and although I never made it to the Science Room or SharpShooters due to being a car-less jit, respect is due to the twin pillars of early 90's Miami Hip Hop.

Along with the lack of press, the live shows featuring established artists were few and far between. In what would become a pattern, shows were relegated to music conferences and holiday weekends. Into this void stepped DJ Raw, who was already in the scene as a record store and label owner. After watching news coverage of the 1994 Woodstock festival, he and Omar Islam, a founding member of the Miami Zulu Nation, decided to remix it for the hip hop heads in the bottom, and thus Hoodstock was born.

Raw explains that in a larger sense, it was a reaction to the radio stations. "If they had an event, we would come with the hip hop. They didn't want us, they only wanted the booty guys." But the blueprint had already been laid out by MC Shan: "Hip hop was set out in the dark/they used to do it out in the park." With traditional venues closed to them, Raw and his crew said, "Let's do an event, and this is how we let Miami know that we're here."

The first Hoodstock, on Columbus Day weekend in 1994, had approximately two thousand heads in attendance. But in 1995, the "How Can I Be Down?" music conference raised the stakes. Looking to get in the industry door, Raw took a meeting in order to try to get a performance slot. With their resumé consisting of Rock Steady Anniversary and B-Boy Summit appearances, the Knock Out Posse was about to take a body blow. "Peter Thomas, Russell Simmons…these guys teamed up and they came down here to basically rape South Florida," remembers Raw. "They milked the shit out of the industry, promised all these dreams they couldn't uphold."

The meeting proved to be an eye-opener in the ways of the industry. "It's going to be $50,000 and we're going to put you in the amateur stage," Raw says he was told by a HCIBD? rep. He was incredulous: "That just rubbed me the wrong way. I'm from Miami, none of you guys are from here." He asked: "You're gonna come to Miami and regulate the industry, then you want me to give you fifty grand?"

The underhanded tactics lit a spark in Raw and his associates in the KOP. His response to the amateur stage booking fee was "We're gonna do a major event in the inner city, you could stay here on the beach with this yuppie shit you got going." Thus, he served notice to HCIBD's plans. "We're gonna do a free event running parallel to your event." A subsequent conversation between DJ Raw and Thomas set the precedent for future Hoodstock productions as the HCIBD? team focused on catering to the industry. Calling in assistance from the Rock Steady Crew, Hoodstock was able to secure free performances from Channel Live, Fat Joe, and others.

I was still deep in the scene, and lamenting the fact that all this output and creative expression in the 305 was neither seen nor heard outside Dade County. In 1997 (Year of the Jiggy), I resolved to remedy this. I had no idea how or with whom, but the idea took hold after I saw yet another *Source* magazine fashion spread set in South Beach.

Closer to home, The [Check]Point hip hop store relocated to Southwest 122nd Avenue and Coral Way in Tamiami, as my family had done as well. In fact, I now lived directly behind The Point and would cop tapes and shirts. In a few months, they shut down for good as the owners were also selling weed out the back. Other stores like The Backway and Crazy Goods in Kendall and Flava Station in downtown ran a cleaner shop, but most heads like myself were in their late teens/early twenties and were spending what little pocket money we had on blunts and getting into Club Zippers. Meanwhile, the club scene in the beach was transforming into a playground for the established artists and their weed dealers.

DJ Coop D Vill at "The Zoo" 1993

By now, the scene was so large that *The Herald* had to make it a cover story on the eve of the 1996 Hoodstock and HCIBD?. I was geeked as I devoured the article. Rol-Up from Flava Station was featured*: "His store, specializing in hip hop clothing that includes a signature line, opened Thursday. The shop is designed to look like a subway station on New York's F" line from Brooklyn to Queens. It's big and airy with lots of aluminum piping, columns and graffiti art, and strategically located across the street from Miami-Dade Community College's downtown Wolfson campus." "The store is chock full of the elements of hip hop, including the Flava/Rol-Up gear: oversize T-shirts, baggy jeans, hooded sweatshirts, brightly colored dresses, baseball caps and backpacks. Prices range from $12 to $250." Although the article and location brought an initial boost, eventually he had to close up shop as sales dwindled. Roland "Rol-Up" Jaramillo remained on the scene for years, hosting and promoting parties, clubs, networking, managing artists, making the orange encircled "F" a bat-signal for hip hop, and becoming a South Florida legend before his untimely passing on May 19th, 2015.

From the seed planted by Jimmy Henchmen and Peter Thomas in the inaugural 1993 HCIBD? Convention, a strange and mutated fruit would grow in the form of a hedonistic capitalist spectacle. In the pre-internet Stone Age, aside from the monthly magazines, there was a network of independent newsletters and fanzines. I had gotten a hold of one by the Bomb Hip Hop Shop in

---

* Burch, Audra D.S. "S. FLORIDA TAKES ITS PLACE IN HIP HOP NATION." *Miami Herald* 14 Oct. 1996, Final ed., Business Monday sec. *Access World News.* Web. infoweb. newsbank.com/resources/doc/nb/news/0EB4D5AE7A24E631?p=AWNB

the Bay Area, and they wrote about the Gavin and Jack The Rapper conventions where lyricists congregated and legendary MC battles took place.

Meanwhile, we had to put up with violence, including shootouts, at Heavy D and Biggie shows on South Beach during the 1996 edition of HCIBD?. Incredibly, *The Herald* lobbied for the convention to remain on the beach, citing the "$2 million in business" generated over Columbus Day weekend, violence be damned. This after they ran the following report[**]:

"Hoodstock, Dade's only inner city hip-hop festival, took place Sunday at Roberto Clemente Park, 101 NW 34th St. Run by Wynwood natives Raul Medina and Peter Price of Knock Out Productions, the third annual free festival drew about 40 acts. There is no official attendance record, though Price estimated the crowd at about 1,000. The How Can I Be Down? music convention on South Beach, run by concert promoter Peter Thomas, drew more than 7,000 people and a few million dollars to South Beach. In its wake, the city was left with trashed hotel rooms and stickers on city light poles and trash cans. At a Sunday night concert at South Beach's Rezurrection Hall, a security guard was shot. There were so many complaints that Miami Beach gave the concert the boot. How Can I Be Down? is not welcome next year, city officials said."

Thankfully, the Miami Beach city commission prevailed over *The Herald's* editorial stance and Peter Thomas had to take his conference to Montego Bay, Jamaica. Even though the Herald quoted

---

[**] Herald Staff, ed. "STAND-OFF OVER HIP HOP." *Miami Herald* 17 Oct. 1996, Final ed., Editorial sec. *Access World News*. Web. infoweb.newsbank.com/resources/doc/nb/news/0EB4D5AFDD4F124B?p=AWNB

Yonis Quintero

Miami Police Lieutenant Mario Garcia as saying that Hoodstock was "quiet, not one problem,"*** news would later emerge that would ruin the best hip hop event Miami ever had.

Around this same time, the Miami Zulu Nation entered a period of turmoil and soon disbanded. Inspired by the founding principles, a couple of heads from Kendall who were regulars at meetings decided to found a new organization. Calling it 360 Productions, it had a more scholarly tip. Much like the 5 Percenters and Nation of Islam, lessons were typed up and handed out at meetings. I signed up and it was through attending meetings that I met some great friends that I am close to to this day, and others that joined the staff of my brainchild: The Cipher - Miami's Hip Hop Newspaper.

Nearby, another organization was also rising from the ashes of the UZN. Planet Earth Productions was headed by Godfree and was focused on the cultural elements of hip hop. A young DJ who started off as Lucky Luciano and then changed his moniker to Battlekat was putting out mixtapes on the local level but with a lot of flavor. I was also doing my part: I found an open spot on MDCC Kendall's radio station, 1600 AM, and was granted a two-hour slot from 5-7 p.m. on Thursdays. Maybe only ten people heard the signal, but let me tell you those ten listeners were treated to Organized Konfusion, Outkast, Jedi Mind Tricks, Dr. Octagon, and a slew of other underground sounds.

*** Lynch, Marika. "HOODSTOCK BRINGS PEACE, ENTERTAINMENT TO WYNWOOD." *Miami Herald* 17 Oct. 1996, Final ed., Neighbors NC sec. *Access World News*. Web. infoweb.newsbank.com/resources/doc/nb/news/0EB4D5AECBB213C4?p=AWNB.

'93

THE PHATEST HIP-HOP FASHIONS FROM N.Y, PHILLY, CALI

MIXED TAPES MAGAZINE5

POSTERS

Manzer Siddique

While Miami celebrated the Marlins winning their first World Series and ending the championship drought, '97 gave way to 1998 (Year of The Cipher). The universal, metaphysical, spiritual, lyrical miracle, whatever you want to call it, was drawing us together to give birth to a local publication that represented Miami and its artists, writers, MCs, DJs, B-boys and B-Girls, promoters, anyone and everyone who claimed and lived hip hop. As I was active in 360 Productions and wanted to cover all aspects of the culture, the name "Cipher" seemed like a natural fit. Just as a cipher of MCs or B-Boys/B-Girls gather in a circle to battle and outwit each other, and DJs spin circular vinyl creating grooves, the publication aimed to center around heads that wanted to represent Miami in the written form since no one was doing it for us.

In late '97, the cultural split was in full swing. The mixtape scene was flooded with DJ Clue? clones, while mainstays like Tony Touch and Ron G were adapting to the times by featuring Foxy Brown and Mase. Meanwhile, the underground "independent as fuck" movement was coming into its own. Vinyl was now available at The Backway and Spec's South Beach, where I had gotten a job and felt like I died and went to heaven twice over. I would clock out of work at midnight and casually stroll across the parking lot to Club Cream or Zen, where DJ Epps was holding it down.

The Miami scene was changing as well. Raul "DJ Raw" Medina Jr., the founder and promoter of Hoodstock, was arrested for running a cocaine distribution ring on September 16th, 1997. What was already common knowledge in the underground burst onto the front page of the Herald and the 5 o'clock news.

"Medina and his wife, Maria, were among 23 people arrested in the culmination of a year-long trafficking investigation," the newspaper reported. "Police said the loosely organized group distributed five to ten kilograms of cocaine a week in Dade and Broward. Their inner workings were captured on court-ordered wiretaps and surveillance videos." After years of his name ringing out in Wynwood, the law caught up to DJ Raw.

"It was just to bring something positive to the area of Wynwood" he said in front of the news cameras as he was cuffed and led away, and this a mere two weeks before Hoodstock '97. Follow-up stories with headlines like: "The Rise and Fall of a Legend in the Hood," "Good Guy Gone Bad or Great Pretender," and "Happenings in the Hood Dashes Dade's Hip Hop Dreams" cemented his reputation with the public. However, hip hop heads appreciated what Hoodstock meant and what it stood for, regardless of the personal failings of its founder.

After this debacle and the industry takeover of South Beach, the time had come to take the torch and make our mark. With no publishing experience and no rap industry connections whatsoever, how could we manifest our dreams into reality? The idea and the desire was there, and I always paid attention to Masta Ace's sign on the door: no biting allowed. This line from "The Symphony" is hip hop rule number one. At this same exact time, we in 360 got a hold of a PEP newsletter where they were putting out a call for writers for a "Miami Hip Hop newsletter." This was it! I contacted them immediately and let them know I was down for the cause.

Godfree of Planet Earth Productions then introduced me to Cristina, one of their members and the one who had the idea for the newsletter. We hit it off cool, but I wanted to expand it beyond a simple newsletter. As far as I knew, the only publications that bothered with Miami Hip Hop were *Freeground*, of which I only got my hands on one issue, and a b&w graffiti zine called Miami Method that showcased the numerous pieces throughout the city. Professionally, 12ozProphet had launched in 1995 and its slick color pages were blessed with piece after piece. They were focused on graffiti and rightfully so, as their first editorial made clear: "Now Miami can be properly represented as not just a place for jacking tourists and listening to booty bass, but as a place with skills that can flow ill styles."

I wanted to do the same for the hip hop scene in general. I was aware of the "fuck booty bass" sentiment, but disagreed completely. Some heads wanted to get as far away from Miami Bass as possible, they felt it gave us a bad name as it was just chant after chant at 120 bpm without displaying any real lyrical skill. I argued that it was our contribution to hip hopthe whole world knew who the 2 Live Crew and the Ghetto Style DJs were and where they hailed from. It was party music that got the girls doing hydraulics and the guys hyped... who could hate on that?

Don't you wanna dance to the Uncle Al song? 1998 presented us with the following: The Gates was long gone—DJ Craze had moved on to prepare to win the first of his three DMC World Champion titles. The Zulu Nation was dormant, and there was even a gang from Broward County claiming the name. On the radio front, WDNA had moved to an all-jazz format and that meant the end of the Saturday Night Funk Box. The farewell show was a hodgepodge of freestyles and B-sides, heads calling in, and the Rhythm Rocker signing off the airwaves, marking the end of an era.

However, the demise of WDNA and the Hip Hop Shop with Darnella (she graduated from UM and took a position at WEDR 99 Jamz, our "blazin' Hip Hop and R&B" Hot 97 clone) opened the airwaves to pirate radio stations, a godsend to heads starved for that new shit. Seemingly overnight, 97.7 FM from Liberty City broadcast DJ Uncle Al shouting out hoods and schools, 96.9 Beach FM brought the electronic sounds, MTA 94.5 FM from downtown broadcast hip hop, and DJ Raw plus the Hoodstock crew put the signal out on WJHH (We Just Hip Hop) 91.7 FM from a mobile studio on a bus.

But the granddaddy of them all, the one with the strongest signal, and the one that could be heard all over Miami broadcast from their base in North Miami Beach: Mixx 96.1 FM, which focused on dance-hall and soca, but had given DJ Khaled the weekday after school and rush hour slot. My man was killing 'em! Big Pun, Outkast, Redman, Wu-Tang, etc. were getting daytime unedited radio play. After only a few months, the majors (Power 96 and 99 Jamz) started to take note when they saw their ratings dip. Who wants to listen to Slammin' Felix Sama (no disrespect) when the Palestinian Rebel was playing the uncut version of "Triumph" at 4 p.m.? Having migrated down from Orlando in '95 (coincidence?), DJ Khaled had Dade County in a headlock. No question, he had to be featured.

Unfortunately, the pirate radio scene fell victim to the same familiar Miami ill: beef, shit talking, and drama. It led to wars over advertisers and frequencies—eventually the FCC had to get involved when the major stations started complaining. Perhaps in a bid to gain listeners, it didn't help that Mixx 96 was right next to Power 96 on the dial. Raids, confiscation of transmitters, and snitches kept the pirates on the run. You might tune in hoping to hear the latest record only to be greeted by static. Expensive transmitters and equipment were stolen or locked away by the feds. The end was swift and unexpected. Tragically, DJ Uncle Al was murdered in Liberty City on September 10th, 2001 due to a beef with another crew over equipment and frequencies. Today, pirates broadcast intermittently, with Mixx 96 and 97.7 "Peace In The Hood" re-launched as legal community stations after having survived the late 90's radio wars.

PART :2

THE CIPHER: MIAMI'S HIP HOP NEWSPAPER

By March of 1998, I had had enough of Miami being overlooked and decided to put together the first issue. I had no clue as to how to do that, but I was determined. After having made contact with Cristina Solana and the Planet Earth Productions crew, I started gathering information and contacting heads I knew for interviews. Obviously Khaled was on the list, so I reached out through Godfree and we arranged to meet at the Mixx 96 broadcast studio in North Miami Beach. I already knew him from the scene, so my first interview went smooth and I wrote it up:

> In the Mixx 96 studios you won't find a glamorous radio station setup. What you will see are some dedicated brothers and sisters doing their thing for self and defying authority, which is really the whole point of Hip Hop anyway. For example, on the day I visited, DJ Craze was in the house spinning underground records. Company Flow and The Arsonists at three in the afternoon! Beautiful.

> Taking some time out from his hectic schedule (The Temple is only two nights away at the time of this writing) Khaled spoke to me about his operation. As for the early days and getting put on, the brother came up the old school way: straight up hustling. "How I came up was the streets with

DJ Khaled

Juan Galan (Off the Hook Promotions) and DJ Khaled

DJ Khaled

my crew The Hitmen, Nasty and Caesar out of Orlando; as in we just kept throwin' parties and parties and parties," he said. "About me getting a radio show was just straight up selling myself, letting brothers know what the deal is and like: yo, I'm not here to play! And they gave me a chance and it was just on!"

Having previously played at New Orleans' WTUL Tulane University and Orlando's WPRK Rollins College underground mix shows, Khaled has the experience needed to rock Miami five days a week. With the eternal underground vs. commercial debate still raging, he's trying not to get caught in the middle. "I don't consider myself commercial cuz we playin' what the people want." Khaled points out. "If I'm in the streets I know what the people want and it's the best feeling in the world, knowing people's feeling you every day."

Obviously the Miami scene has grown since his arrival two years ago. So what does he think of the vibe in the bottom? "Hip Hop at this time right now when people coming, it's something to do, it's something we gonna make happen" he stated. "I think Miami is definitely gonna be the spot because people come to visit no matter what. If it's not for music reasons, it's for vacation." No doubt the 305 is always live, but eventually player haters have to rear their ugly heads. His opinion? "It's like different brothers out here that's doing stuff is doing it the way it's supposed to be done, but there's also brothers out there that's making it bad for brothers. You know how it is, playa hatin and all that!"

Certainly this disease has gotten out of control. I'm sure you've heard the comments of individuals dissin' and talkin' shit. I myself used to be one of these misguided souls, not really knowing what was going on behind the scenes. According to Khaled, the reason is "jealous ones envy, just plain and simple. Not just Miami, not just with Khaled. Everywhere you go you gonna run into that, that's life. I mean, put it this way: only the strong survive."

But what about the negative vibe in Hip Hop? The records promoting violence, materialism, and disrespect of females? Does this really influence people, like some outsiders claim? Khaled takes a firm pro-freedom of speech stance. "I can never disrespect anybody's vibe cuz I ain't nobody to tell what they wanna say or how they wanna say it. Now, as in influencing people, I don't think it is, because people should be strong enough to know it's music." That's right, Republicans.

After the success of the last two Temple parties, you didn't think he was actually gonna stop, did you? Matter of fact, check what he's got in store: "We got this KRS tour coming that On Point is throwing and it's the whole state of Florida. They put four DJ's from Miami down on that, to go with KRS, Funkmaster Flex, and Tony Touch on tour." Should be fresh, especially since it's the bottom's own. As for the haters, heed his last words: "All the devils out there can never stop this."

After the success of that article, thinking that it was actually easy (was I in for a big surprise!), the idea came to me to feature the four elements of hip hop. For the dance section, who better than B-Girl Beta, who was fifteen years old at the time and already taking suckers out. Far from a novelty, she had genuine skills and broke the chickenhead stereotype. For the rapper article, there was a wealth of MCs opening up for national acts such as Da Alliance, B-Dope, Mic Rippa, and others. The previous generation that had rocked on the Saturday Night Funk Box had moved on, with the exception of B-Dope from the Laststrawze. In the end I decided to go with Pee-Do, Godfree's cousin who was also deep in the scene. Finally, for the graffiti component, a young writer by the name of Sane from RME crew handled the intro. Today, he's the internationally acclaimed fine artist Alvaro Ilizarbe aka Freegums.

I sat down and formatted the issue, laying it out on cardboard via cutting and pasting Microsoft Word 98™ printouts from MDCC (give thanks.) Masthead, table of contents, edi-borial, features, poetry, plus the usual music reviews. I didn't want to cover what everyone was already talking about in the first quarter of '98 (The Lox, Silkk The Shocker, and DMX), so I chose the underground backpacker and local MC route.

Along with not having the first clue as to cutting and pasting layout, I was also faced with another dilemma: where and how to print it? Thankfully, Cristina came through with a printing plant she knew of in Hialeah. Unfortunately, she had other responsibilities and left the staff. I continued to put together the first issue. From the beginning, we were low budget, or no budget really, since we had no investors, no backing, nothing of that sort. I still wanted to put out a quality product, but one trip to the plant showed me that color printing was out of the question. The lowest color print run was about two thousand copies and cost twice that. So the decision was made to go with b&w newsprint, all I could afford.

With the Miami Hip Hop economy up and running in the form of clothing shops, record stores, and indie labels, these were natural targets for advertising. Business plan? Press kit? Audience projections? What's that? All I did was walk into the establishments and sell my dream. It helped that there was no local competition and the national rags were out of reach, budget wise. I secured commitments for a three-issue ad buy and had checks in my hand. There was no going back now. Those first advertisers paid for the initial thousand copy print run.

When yours truly was arranging *The Cipher*'s first issue, there was only one thing on every hip hop head's mind: The Temple. A party promoted by DJ Khaled, it took its name from the first location where it was held: The Mahi Shrine Auditorium off River Drive in Allapattah (now demolished to make way for Miami River Landing, a mixed-use condo development.) At the time, it was the local headquarters of the Shriners, the somewhat "secret society" fraternity affiliated with the Freemasons and best known for its nonprofit children's hospital network.

With his daily mix show covering nearly the entire South Florida metro area, Khaled promoted the second Temple party

B-Boy Masters Pro-Am—1999

Miami B-Boy Representatives at the Rock Steady Crew
21st Anniversary battle in NYC—1998

as "South Bronx invades South Beach" with Fat Joe and Big Pun headlining at Club Onyx (now a Miami Beach Public Library branch). It seemed as though every night Godfree and his PEP crew could be seen promoting up and down Washington and Collins in South Beach, handing out thousands of flyers. It got to the point where in order to stand out, they needed picket signs and bullhorns to drown out all the other promoting crews. The Temple promised to be the party to end all parties, and with "Twinz '98" getting constant play plus Pun's up and coming reputation as the next hot MC, every head in Dade and beyond knew where to be on the night of March 6th.

That night, as Godfree, PEP, and I left from the meet up spot in the Hammocks shopping plaza on Southwest 147th Avenue and Killian Drive in Kendall, thoughts turned to the fact that this would become my first official job as a journalist. On the personal front, I was finishing up credits at MDCC Kendall, intending to transfer to FIU, while working nights at Spec's Music in South Beach (Now a Walgreens thanks to MP3s and iTunes). I now had an actual tangible project to be published. The challenge for me was to not make it another "hip hop show" article: "the MC rocked the stage, the audience was hype, blah blah blah…" Little did I know it was to be anything but.

Arriving at the spot, the crowd that had lined up down the block was something I had never seen before. With the amount of people trying to get in, it was as if they were giving money away inside. We made our way to the front of the line and got introduced to the age-old Miami tradition: "Naaahh…don't see your name on the list." How quickly they forget. Never mind all the nights the crew spent promoting on the beach, all the shoutouts on the radio, all the flyers passed out. Bouncers are always quick to let the females in but to front like work wasn't put in was not the thanks PEP and I expected.

However, before smartphones and Twitter, word of mouth was the social network. Huddling up, it was agreed to send word to Khaled that we were out front and not going away. Chances were a snowball in hell odds that he would come out. Fortunately for us, the bouncers were overwhelmed by the crushing amount of people, so we just slid in right under their noses in a split second as they were trying their best to maintain crowd control. Second industry lesson learned: persistence pays off.

Once inside, the scene was thick, the club packed to capacity bordering on a fire hazard. It was a hodgepodge of sweating, bumping shoulders, "excuse me," "damn girl!" giving pounds and handshakes, "yo! What's the deal?!?" watch out, don't step on any sneakers, oh shit that's the homie, "what up what up!?" After navigating the length of the club, we finally made it to the makeshift side stage which was brilliantly positioned to get a bird's eye view of the show. Once again security stood in our path, but flashing a homemade press pass made the blockade part. As for the party itself, the first issue of The Cipher gave the reader the scoop:

> After all the hype, advertising, and brothers promoting with picket signs, did The Temple deliver the goods? Well, let's just say that everything that coulda happened, did. From turntablism to freestyles to chickens clucking to

Cipher Zine GRAFF page on Top.
roskis © IH

Chris Mendoza

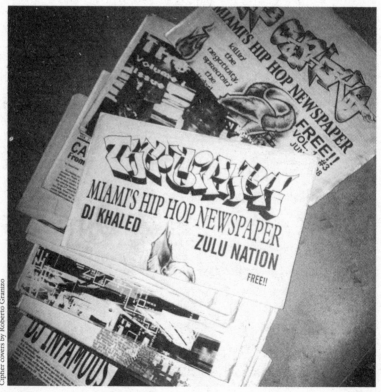

girls getting eaten out on stage to windows being smashed, March 6th was off the hook!

Onyx security trying to front like I ain't on the list? No problem, just walk right in under their noses without saying a word. Bouncers backstage denying my press credentials? No big deal. Just kick some game and I'm in. First up: Khaled getting the crowd hype. You know his steez. Next: DJ Craze on some turntablist beat juggle flares cuts to leave your mouth hanging open. Then: Tony Toca had you screaming esa loca! On the M.I.C. two kids whose name I forgot (my bad) opened up but dissed the crowd, therefore no love. Finally, Terror Squad came on.

Fat Joe, Big Punisher, and Cuban Link delivered a solid performance. They had energy and managed to get the crowd open, plus the Latin vibe was strong while they represented lovely. However, Big Pun must not ever lift up his shirt again, no matter if he's getting his freak on with a groupie.

Well, that did it. The first issue of *The Cipher* went out soon after and it hit Miami with the force and strength of a Category 4 hurricane. The final touch was, of course, the cover, clearly the most important aspect in my eyes. Through Sane I met another brilliant artist, Honest Benevolent, who contributed the piece that adorned the front cover while my man Nok 9 drew *"The Cipher"* title. Later on, Honest would come on board as the official graphic designer, but we'll get to that.

Regardless of cost, The Cipher went out to every high school, college campus, barbershop, record store, club, and venue we could find. The rest of the industry was jigged out to the max, while the backpacker underground was mad. Although I was partial to Company Flow and Hieroglyphics, I didn't want the paper to be all about that. The feedback we were getting from heads in MIA was overwhelmingly positive. Of course, there were a few haters: "why is it not in color?" "Why don't you interview DMX?" and things of that nature. But we pressed on, starting work on the second issue.

Cristina returned to the fold and we agreed to divide up labor as follows: She agreed to secure the sponsors and advertisers, while I handled the editorial section. Pretty soon we found that word had spread beyond Dade. We received a call from that faraway planet known as Broward County from the incomparable Heather Bee. A down by law hip hop head from Coral Springs, she came armed with camera skills and connections in place. Of course we needed a photographer, especially one who had just come back from a Vibe magazine festival at Pleasure Island in Orlando with a ton of pics.

As the late 90's Miami Hip Hop scene progressed, I began to identify two different kinds of artists: the ones trying (and failing) to make it in the industry and the ones that didn't care about deals and were just doing their thing. As with most scenes, the more talented ones chose the second route, wanting to express themselves and their art in the most natural way possible, free from the pressure of trying to get on. As the national hip hop scene split into the jiggy vs. backpacker camps, so did Miami. Actual backpackers were few and far between, but the hip hop "culture" "four elements" "true school" scene was massive in the 305. Of course, the jiggy South Beach crowd outnumbered us, so I tried to create a balance in our coverage. But as a book loving 21-year-old, I wanted to be uplifting and party at the same time.

For example, I went to a couple of shows by signed industry rappers and this is how I saw it:

Consider this the introduction to my long awaited book entitled "Why The Rap Industry Is Wack." On the 16th of April, the one-man catalog Cappadonna passed through on his "Pillage" promo tour [*at club Cream, which is shuttered now*]. Being that he wasn't clockin' much loot, his show was brief and to the point. But that's what happens when labels that are only interested in the bottom line need to promote newly signed artists, who then have to go platinum to recoup.

But you don't care about that. So I'll just tell you about the performance: The swarm came on early, about 1:30 AM or so (Remember, this is Miami—we don't get out of bed to go clubbing before 2 AM). Heads had fun with slang editorials and reciting 2 minute Winter Warz verses acapella. Unfortunately, the fun came to an end quickly, as Cappa bowed and let fans get on stage and freestyle. The rest of us were left asking "That's it?"

Backstage was where the fun was just getting started. Groupie selections for each crew member had begun and there was no way I was going to get an interview. So I

grabbed my trusty female friend and made my way past the bone crushers guarding the entrance. Here's what I found: Free Alizé all around, but I stay dry. Beautiful honeys seeking hotel access, but I'm not a rapper. Bored, I called it a night and broke out.

So there you have it, a night in the life of a rap star. Think about the fact that they have to do this all over the country and in some cases, the world. So now you know what to tell them clueless fools who ask, "why are they so angry?"

That was my mad writer article for Cappadonna's quickie promo show. It helped that I was working at Spec's Music in South Beach and could just cross the parking lot (it's the Wells Fargo/CVS/parking garage retail complex now) and talk my way into Club Cream. Later, Heather got tight with the owners and we just strolled in at will for any event. Around the same time, we covered a Beatnuts show:

I don't get it: despite their popularity in the bottom, attendance to this show was the lowest I've ever seen. Probably cuz of poor promotions (I didn't see a flyer til 3 days before the jam), not a lot of heads got down with deez 'Nuts. But The Cipher was there and now we bring you the goods.

After being warmed up by that Guatauba kid, Tony Touch, (who shocked the hell out of me when he played Hector Lavoe in the middle of his set) the crowd was amped for the show. Wait, chill for a sec: Here comes Mic Rippa to open up. He had energy and did come off the head, but heads was on some skeptical shit. Following a brief intermission, the Junkyard and Psycho Les emerged on stage.

Ju-Ju straight up went for broke. In true Hip Hop fashion, he gave the audience their money's worth. Psycho Les wasn't really that hyped, but didn't disappoint either. However, his partner was going bonkers rippin all the hits: "Find That," "Do You Believe," "Reign of The Tec," and "Off The Books" ignited the crowd. Afterwards, he was acting like nothing happened, just chillin like normal. Rockin' for about 45 minutes or so, they chanted their life's goals: fuck, drink beer, and smoke some shit. Then they broke out for the hotel with the party caravan.

In contrast to the signed rappers and their hangers-on, I had also got into the rave scene. My first one was at Club Salvation on 17th Street and West Avenue (now an Office Depot). Nok 9 and I rolled up that night to find a line full of ravers and I remember thinking, "where are all these people from?" cuz it was the stereotypical pacifier/JNCO parachute jeans/multiple wild piercings crowd. But the reason we went was DJs Coop D Vill and Craze were spinning. Turns out the club had multiple rooms, one of which was the hip hop area. The two Tekmasters spun Mos Def, The Roots, Redman, and others as we geeked out to records that you couldn't hear anywhere else in Miami. We explored the other rooms as well and I was mind-blown: I became a full-fledged raver after that, just without the clothes and drugs. It was all about the music for me: hip hop, drum'n'bass, breaks, and downtempo. Outkast, Roni Size, DJ Baby Anne, and Portishead. Gang Starr, Andy C, DJ Icey, and Massive Attack. Working at Spec's

Slick Rick performing in Miami—1999

was a daily trip to music heaven where I could cop underground vinyl and British imports with my employee discount.

The night after the show at The Temple, I rolled to the Port of Miami for a rave/hip hop show, the Recombinant Music Lounge. Not only was the illbient producer DJ Spooky performing, he was to be joined by Mixmaster Mike & Q-Bert of the Invisibl Skratch Piklz, DJs Babu and Melo-D of the Beat Junkies, Rob Swift and Roc Raida of the X-ecutioners, and DJs Craze and Infamous from the MIA. All of this was going down in a port terminal usually reserved for family-friendly cruise boardings. All aboard! I couldn't believe that these turntable wizards were all performing under one roof, and in Miami.

As I entered the cavernous space, the light shows, strobes, and thumping bass overwhelmed my senses. The turntablists wrecked shop, with Mixmaster Mike severely deconstructing and beat juggling GZA's "4th Chamber" electric guitar intro. Something told me to stick around after the DJs traded routines and mixes. Sure enough, the electronic/experimental room was on fire, with DJ Spooky going all the way left field, mixing jungle breaks with synthesizer loops.

Just knowing that 24 hours prior to this, I was holding on for dear life as Fat Joe and Big Pun smashed their set made this rave that much better since it would be a while before these legendary DJs would come back to the bottom. Again, I was bewildered by the presence of hundreds of kids decked out in full raver gear—it was as if they hibernated and only emerged at night with the baggiest of

JNCO parachute jeans, smedium FreshJive tees, wild multi-colored hair, and chrome chokers.

I wonder now what it would have been like to experience those sounds and the light shows on E or tabs, but alas, I will never know. To me, drugs were a distraction from the talent on stage. I had already quit smoking blunts and was semi-straight edge (I kept a two-drink max at the club, but most nights I didn't sip at all.) As I got deeper into the nightlife, I was offered and was around every controlled substance short of heroin. "Live and let live" was my motto: I witnessed plenty of heads snort lines, drop GHB, get lost in the K-hole, roll balls, and go on acid trips, but I always turned down the invites to join in the mind-altering. To be frank, I was deathly scared of possible brain damage or some shit, so I guess those "this is your brain on drugs" commercials worked on someone.

But I digress. For our second issue, the main theme was the B-Boy Masters Pro-Am, one of a number of dance battles and expos taking place across the country. The year prior, I had attended the inaugural session at Florida International University, where original Miami B-Boy Speedy Legs and his partner Zulu Gremlin put on an exhibit that unfortunately didn't get a lot of press. For this year, legends such as Ken Swift and Frosty Freeze of the Rock Steady Crew were in the house, along with crews from all over the country and overseas.

Needless to say, with heads from various points in attendance, we spread *The Cipher* gospel far and wide. No incidents, no rival crews beefing, no violence, and no fronting, as opposed to the industry events taking place on South Beach throughout the

Tek of Smif-N-Wessun performing—Miami 1998

DJ Craze

year. We were babies in this, just lovers and appreciators of the culture we had grown up in. Now, we had a voice for Miami, from Miami.

Speaking of beef, I caught my first whiff of it when I interviewed DJ Craze, who was already on his way to becoming a legend. He was the only one who had broken out of the local scene and gone national, and at the time of the interview, was starting to go global as well. Having known him since the Zulu Nation meetings in Wynwood and being a regular at The Gates, it was nothing to get him to sit down and answer some questions. Through him, I was introduced to drum'n'bass thanks to an Andy C/Peshay mixtape that he brought back from his first gig in London, and I've been hooked on D&B ever since. At this point, I had already transferred to FIU and was taking a couple of journalism classes, but either I skipped or wasn't paying attention to the part about quotes and context. (Most likely, I slept in and skipped class that day after yet another all-night party bender.)

The interview went smoothly, and like I said, we knew each other. I believe he felt comfortable and spoke to me as if he was talking to one of his boys. He spoke candidly and with no reservations. There was a lot of laughter, and as I transcribed it I remember thinking "damn, he just doesn't give a fuck!" But then again, neither did I. Our agenda was hip hop culture, but since I chose to run the interview verbatim without giving background to his quotes, it came back to bite me in the ass in a major way. Here's an example of a Q&A that went south upon publication:

Omen: how is the underground and commercial industry affecting the scene?

Craze: That's affecting me like a muthafucka cuz ain't nobody booking me in Miami! [Laughter]. Cuz I won't play none of that shit! [More laughter]. So it's affecting a lot of the real Hip Hop heads and shit. A lot of heads ain't got nowhere to go, cuz they ain't trying to dress nice to go to a club, so the commercial shit is fuckin it all up!

Omen: What's the deal with Tekmasters? [Craze's original Miami DJ crew, with DJs NV, Coop D Vill, Infamous, and Fiendish]

Craze: I'm not even gonna front, it was me and NV at first. But NV is more into his job and his girl so it was like whatever… he never came to practice with us and never did shit so we just like, you know? Fuck him or whatever. Now it's just me, Cooper [Coop D Vill], Infamous, and Fiendish. I have all the say in it, but I don't like to say. I leave that shit to NV and Fiendish cuz half the time, I'm not even here, so it's like "ya'll do what ya'll wanna do, just don't fuck up the name" and they keep fuckin' up! [Wild laughter].

To be clear, the "fuck him or whatever" was said in the tone of voice one uses when doing the SMH meme, that sort of exasperated "I can't believe this" type of reaction. Not disrespectful, not insulting. But of course upon reading it in b&w, it looks like it could be starting some shit.

The fallout was swift and immediate. On the same day that the paper came back from the printers, I got a call from an irate Craze: "Yo! WTF are you doing? How you gonna print that? That's fucked up! You gotta get rid of that quote!" I apologized as fast as I could because, as if the quote wasn't bad enough, I had already handed off some copies to Cristina and our staff writer Shareef to distribute. When I told him this, he flipped his shit: "That's fucked up! You gotta get a marker or something and cross out the other copies you got!" Anything to contain the damage. So that's what I did, but of course it was too late. Eventually, it died off with the next issue where I ran a correction, but this was just a preview of what was to come. Although this one was self-inflicted, drama would eventually appear and cast a cloud over the whole operation.

As I said, there was plenty of talent that was not getting any shine outside of the 305. Many MCs were opening for the big acts, rhyming on the radio shows and mixtapes, and at any open mic possible. One of them was Mic Rippa, who had crazy buzz on the scene and was sure to blow up. His single "96 Cream Hunt" produced by Ju-Ju of The Beatnuts, got major play on the pirates and allowed him to open for a lot of the acts that came down to perform. After Mother Superia's industry shakedown, our hopes were placed on the half-Dominican, half-Haitian lyricist working on his debut album with local indie label Rolly Roll Records.

We were left waiting—his long-awaited debut LP was never officially released. He remained on the scene for years: opening for acts, taking out all comers, and occasionally making appearances on mixtapes. Sadly, Steven "Mic Rippa" Dorce passed away on March 2nd, 2013. May he rest in power.

Coming back from the Craze quote fallout, we knew we had to step up our focus. School was about to be out for the summer, which meant more heads looking for something to do. As for me, I was still typing out interviews and articles on Microsoft Word™ at school, then taking the printouts and cutting and pasting them onto the print board in my bedroom. At least I had gifted artists like Sane doing the cover title and writers sending flicks and art in. The theme for the third issue was "Killin the negativity, spreading the light!" so we decided to feature DJ Snowhite, B-Dope, and an in-depth interview with the Boot Camp Clik's Smif & Wessun (going by Cocoa Brovas due to litigation from Smith & Wesson®) and Heltah Skeltah, who were promoting their LPs "Da Rude Awakening" and "Magnum Force."

My man Tino connected me with the promoter G-Smooth, who had been active back in the early 90's and was now coming back from hiatus. G was very accommodating, setting up a time and place to interview Rock and Ruck aka Sean Price (RIP), and they were actually at the time and place he said they would be, which would become a rarity. As for Tek and Steele, it was a total freestyle interview right after their show at Club Onyx. I can't say with certainty, but it seems Steele remembered tagging up my black book at Hoodstock a couple of years back, given the way his eyes lit up when I mentioned the defunct festival.

This became the pattern: find out who was performing when and where, find the person behind the talent (a manager,

Steele of Smif-n-Wessun performing—Miami 1998

promoter, booking agent, PR rep, label hack, anybody that could grant access), keep our eyes and ears open to word on the street, keep up with music, DJs, mixtapes, clubs, radio shows, and who was dissin' who. From this, I started delegating labor: you go to this club, you interview this rapper, you go take pics at this event, I'll review records, you get sponsors, etc. By the fourth issue, it became routine.

Now, most of the industry types had never heard of us and were skeptical—these we had to run game on. Others were of the "any publicity is good publicity" school of thought, and a few slammed the door in our faces, as we were just a bunch of kids making it up as we went along. We weren't a fanzine, even though I was cutting and pasting in my bedroom. We weren't glossy either, and we were free. Free price point and free from any pressure to give a good review or good article. I remember being disgusted at *The Source* debacle with Almighty RSO and how the original staff all resigned—I went from loyal reader to wiping my ass with that rag.

All the other ones I used to read in high school and college had fallen off or stopped altogether. From L.A, *Rap Pages* had gone full glossy and wasn't the same, while *Rap Sheet* had simply vanished. In NY, *Vibe* was more for commercial heads in my opinion. *XXL* and *Blaze* were a few months away with their big budgets, so really we had no comp as far as I was concerned. The ones that I read faithfully and was inspired by were *On The Go* (Philly), *4080* (Bay Area), *Ego Trip* (Manhattan), and *Stress* (Q-boro) while *URB* (LA) and *XLR8R* (The Bay) satisfied my raver needs. However, as time went on each one of those fell prey to budgetary constraints and eventually folded. Meanwhile, I believed in our product and dreamed of going full color glossy one day.

To get there, we had to expand our advertising. From day one we had counted on Crazy Hood Productions, Hair Spa U.S.A. (miraculously still around), and Double Cross Entertainment. It was those three sponsors that paid for the first issue. We picked up a few others for the second and third, but getting over the hump to color proved more and more expensive. Our printer, Continental Printing in Hialeah (still in business—Hialeah is forever) was willing to work with us on our total print run. So we went from a thousand to two thousand and then four thousand for the third and fourth issues, increasing quantity while increasing our quality on a monthly schedule.

I always felt that we should promote and give something back to Miami. DJs, B-Boys and Girls, MCs, and graf writers were getting busy all over the city, and I wanted to cover them all. Obviously that was unrealistic, but we tried. Around this time, a breath of fresh air hit the scene: DJ Snowhite's FaatLand spoken word showcase. Held every Tuesday night at the Marlin Hotel, it brought a soulful down to earth vibe to South Beach. This was the summer of '98, the height of the shiny suit jiggy era, when artists of every stripe suddenly "discovered" Miami and flew down to perform on the regular.

But it wasn't always this way, as Edecsta from legendary graffiti crew The Inkheads recalls: "Miami Beach [in the early 90's] was mostly retirees living there, it wasn't like "Oh hotels!" he says. "So everybody used to go to only a few underground spots that had

Ras Kass performing at the Rock Steady Crew's 21st Anniversary—NYC 1998

J-Ro of Tha Alkaholiks performing at the Rock Steady Crew's 21st Anniversary—NYCh

Tash of Tha Alkaholiks performing at the Rock Steady Crew's 21st Anniversary—NYC 1998

Supernatural with his son—Rock Steady Crew 21st Anniversary—NYC 1998

aerosol art outside like Club Nu. I remember seeing Black Sheep at 5th Street's. Shie [a member of The Inkheads] used to DJ at Society Hill. There were no big clubs, it was mostly old timers hanging out!"

But by the late 90's, the beach was saturated with shows—clubs like Onyx, Zen, Cream, and Liquid were hotspots for hip hop. No longer relegated to the back room, it was now headlining the marquee front and center. Alongside that, the rave scene was massive. I had also "discovered" the Winter Music Conference (which has been held since 1985 and takes place in mid-March) and a whole new world of electronic music opened up. I took to saying that hip hop was my wife and drum'n'bass my mistress.

FaatLand took a different approach. A mainstay of the scene since the early 90's, Snowhite had the props and skills to get down with the best of them. She decided to bring the spoken word and open the mic to everyone. I met up with her at pirate radio station Beach 96.9 FM.

"Forget chillin with the dwarves, Snowhite got other things to do: two shows on Beach Radio 96.9 FM, rocking the occasional club or rave, and producing up and coming acts. As I Rol-Up to Beach Radio on Saturday night, I can only think of all the drama she must've dealt with as a woman in Hip Hop." Surprisingly, she didn't even mention it once during our interview. When it came to the FaatLand, she responded:

That's a really cool thing because that's what I call real Hip Hop and keepin' it real. There's no ego trippin', it's not about how the other one looks or how good is the other one, none of that at all. People are not coming because

Just another night in 90's South Beach

Mic Rippa (RIP) performing in Miami

so and so is there; they're coming cuz it's real and they could be themselves. They're gonna hear music that they normally don't hear. I'm playing a lot of the underground Hip Hop that does not get played. Then MC's get open; they have a live band, and nothing is rehearsed. Might end up battling someone, but it's all out of love. MC's love it, it's what I call a lyrical haven; they can't really do this anywhere else. Also, it's a new thing for poets. I'm trying to combine poetry with MCing because if you think about it, you're a lyricist—you're actually a poet.

Before, this wouldn't be accepted because if you were a poet and you went to a club [where] there were MC's, poets would get scared off because they'd feel that the MC's are not gonna understand that. So I combine both of the things together. I start at 9 'o clock and an MC can go on at like 10, a poet can go up at 11:30 and it's still the same, cuz the band is playing live and it's all about expressing yourself, whether you do it in poetry form or MCin' form.

I was featuring a lot of the local talent, because I feel there's a lot of talent out here and people are not recognizing that. So that was my whole purpose behind the FaatLand. It's to let people know that "Hey, we got this music, we got the local talent, we do have a scene in Miami." And when I'm showcasing it, you never know who's gonna be in the house. You could have somebody from a label, a talent scout. I want MC's to be cool with another group or another MC, because we're all from the same place and we're all trying to do the same thing down here.

The issues of giving shine to the next generation coming up and scene politics were also something I was seeing. With hip hop being based around the crew, the clique, the neighborhood, and so forth, politics were a constant presence. This one didn't like that one, this one said this, that one said that, all of that was being manifested. Snowhite was no stranger to it: "As far as getting in, that's a whole 'nother story cuz to be honest, that has nothing to do with how good you are. The beach is monopolized, not everybody can get in, it's about who you know. So you meet people, make your connections, get your foot in the door, you made it. And once you're in there, you can start bringing in other people."

Notice a trend? A talented DJ that stuck to her principles couldn't catch a break, so she created her own lane. FaatLand was an oasis in the cesspool that South Beach had already become. Eventually, it slowly faded out. DJ Snowhite still does her thing along with some graphic design. But the issues she brought up were affecting other DJs and the scene in general: lack of support for local acts, the monopoly of club bookings, the "it's who you know" politics, and the audience split into commercial vs. underground factions. But wait, it gets worse!

Another soulful brother and mainstay on the wheels of steel was DJ Coop D Vill. Coming up with the Tekmasters, he had been rocking since the mid-80's. However, the politics and behind the scenes issues led him to migrate to the more diverse Bay Area in 1999, where he found his niche and continues to spin. I caught up

DJ Snowhite

DJ Coop D Vill gettin' busy on the congas

with him before his departure and he dropped some jewels—"A lot of people don't know that Miami had a strong Hip Hop scene back in the days." With these words Coop D Vill lets it be known that the elements of the culture were being manifested in the bottom while most of us were crawling along. "It didn't just happen overnight, back then [it] was so many people. This B-Boy, Paco, was like the illest doing the aerial moves. Speedy Legs was around, the Def Force Crew." Unfortunately, there were no books written or movies made, leaving some younger heads unaware of the legacy in South Florida."

After paying dues in the bedroom circuit, Coop was ready to advance to the next level. "It was all through vibes as far as wanting to record your own songs, elevated from making beats on tape decks to turntablism and finally to the production." Coop also remembers a kinder, gentler Miami scene in the late 80's and early 90's. "The people make what Hip Hop is, and back then [they] demanded more of the underground. At that time also there was a lot of positivity being kicked by Brand Nubian, KRS, Tribe Called Quest, Jungle Brothers, groups like that trying to kick knowledge. So a lot of that was affecting." Around this time, he started spinning in spots such as The Kitchen Club in Coconut Grove where he lived, with DJ Chris The Power Enforcer on the righteous tip, for "The Zoo" hip hop nights, never forgetting the roots and culture: "The DJ's rotated between me, Epps, [and] Chris. We brought Craze at 14 years old to battle. That was one of the first battles where he showed his stuff in front of a crowd, in a club he wasn't even old enough to be in!" Along with The Sugar Shack, The Zoo was one of the very first club nights that was dedicated to hip hop at a time when Miami

Bass and freestyle dominated the city. Cooper, as he is affectionately known, stuck to his craft and progressed to the next level in the game: production. The process of linking up with other heads to form the Florida Room team was as Miami as it gets: "Through DJ Chris, they all lived in the same area. So I linked up with Harold from the Florida Room production crew. I would take a bus from Coconut Grove all the way to North Miami, go to their house and make beats, collabo with these guys. We had ideas, we would sit down and make something, create magic in a short amount of time. We had chemistry." After producing for local MC's such as Mic Rippa, the Florida Room crew disbanded and Coop departed for the greener chronic on the West Coast. The difference between South Florida and NorCal was night and day. "When I got there and I saw the DJ's, the crowd was definitely different than I was used to. Not just ethnically, but culturally as well. The community of DJ's, the record scene, [and] the vinyl scene was really big for digging for records. That's what really got me into the Bay Area, the amount of knowledge about these records, but also how much of these records there were." Historically, one of the biggest and most established scenes in the country, The Bay welcomed him with open arms:

When Blackstar came out, Rawkus Records, people weren't hip to that. The DJs were, the crowd wasn't. So that was a new thing for them, new music that I was bringing from the East Coast. It was a DJ culture and the Hip Hop culture as a whole, at that time it was really, really solid. The reggae also, cuz of my friend Jah Yzer, transplant from Miami as well. Between those two things there was a lot of work. I got to DJ with my mentors, people I looked up to: Jazzy Jeff, Cash Money, Red Alert, Afrika Bambaataa.

On the other hand, *The Cipher* was just getting some momentum. By the fourth issue, I had a clear idea of what our mission was: a record of what was happening in the scene, interviews with national acts, expanding our advertiser network, and most importantly, getting the name out there. Every show was an opportunity to get the paper prominently displayed on stage. Every shoutout, every record and clothing store placement, every radio show mention, it all mattered. However, the layout left much to be desired. I was still cutting and pasting on Word 98, experimenting with different fonts (and failing since I had zero graphic design skills), the infamous Clippy assistant giving me fits, the blue screen of death, and floppy disks that were always running out of storage space.

But another front was opening up: the Internet. In the dial-up era, it was mostly text and simple graphics that made it online via Netscape Navigator. We had that covered, but no money for a proper website. In that spirit, we linked up with a South Florida online pioneer: The View From Below, which was run by Bronz. He had a website up and running already so we offered him our content in exchange for a monthly column, and thus we could be found on www.thescenes.com/cipher. Of course I wanted a website of our own, but that would have to wait. In the AOL 3.0, free CD in the mail era, I was just happy to have a corner in cyberspace.

The nascent online hip hop domain was concentrated around a few message boards and the AOL Hip Hop chat room. Somewhere in the depths and dungeons of the cyber world,

Godfree had linked up with a couple of hip hop heads from San Diego: GZ and SaSe. In a foreshadowing of his future as a premiere video game podcaster (subscribe to GamerTag Radio now!), he found a long distance access code from a now bankrupt and out of business major toy store. To this day, I don't know exactly how he got the cheat code: Don't ask, don't tell. Those digits enabled him to call any long distance number and talk for as long as he wanted. Unlimited minutes on deck! The payphones on 147th and Killian in The Hammocks became a hotspot, with him and a few other heads hanging out. He put me on to the west coast B-girls and soon I was also using the cheat. Thanks, aforementioned major toy store for all you did for hip hop culture in Miami!

Quite militant, I was one hundred percent keep-it-real hip hop culture. By this point, my college studies had fallen by the wayside. I was getting a bit of shine from the paper and was becoming known in the scene. Feeling like Carlito Brigante when he gets sprung from prison (Completely rehabilitated, reinvigorated, reassimilated!), my staff and I continued to work on our fourth issue. Once again, the reception upon release was better than we could have asked for, but I knew we hadn't arrived yet. That would change in the summer of '98, for at the end of July staff member Shareef and I decided to make our pilgrimage to Mecca and attend the Rock Steady Crew's 21st anniversary in New York City.

I had never been to the rotten apple before, but having listened to hip hop all my life, I had the tools to navigate the 5 boroughs. Thanks to Jeru, I knew to steer clear of homicide central: East New York, where the "manic-depressive psycho murderers"

Plan Beats crew

stalk. Queensbridge is not only the place where stars are born, but according to Nas and Mobb Deep, it gets hectic. Google Maps on wax was how we learned about the slums of Shaolin, Harlem World, The Boogie Down Bronx, Crooklyn, South Side Jamaica, Bed-Stuy: Do or Die, Brownsville: Never Ran, Never Will, The L.E.S, and El Barrio: Spanish Harlem. The sounds from the underground were directing us to Fat Beats, Bobbito's Footwork, and Fat Joe's Halftime. We wanted to do it all but limited time and even more limited funds kept us on the 4 train and confined to lower Manhattan.

The trip from Miami started with us getting dropped off at the La Cubana bus terminal in Allapattah, and it turned out to be a 36-hour ordeal up the corridor. Stops in Orlando, Savannah, North Cakalaka, DC, Philly, Newark, and finally, Washington Heights where it was La Hora de Bailar with Sandy y Papo. Through the MIA-New Yorken grapevine I had heard of a hostel on 103rd and Amsterdam in the Upper West Side. We took a cab, and upon arrival, found that it was the stereotypical backpacker trustafarian college white boy dreads hacky sack type spot. Perfect!

We stashed our bags and hit the pavement, already knowing we have to hit Fat Beats and Bobbito's in the Village. The underground record store was all that we expected and more: vinyl from all the acts I had heard about, CDs and tapes, DJ Riz on the wheels of steel, and can't forget the grand tradition of struggle rappers accosting you on the way in and out with "check me out son, check my shit, got this CD..." It was all a little too close to Gang Starr's skit at the beginning of Hard To Earn: "suckas be coming up to me on some bullshit, talking about they wanna freestyle and shit...breath stinkin like a muthafucka, spittin and shit" on and on. We then made our way to Bobbito's Footwork basement spot, where he was just chillin with t-shirts and kicks for sale. Again, we were in the financial struggle too. Either buy a shirt or buy dinner. Picking up a flyer, we saw that the Lyricist Lounge was going on that night at Wetlands and the cover was only five dollars. We're there: no question. On the mic were Thirstin Howl III, High & Mighty, Scratch, and surprise guest Black Thought. Fuck! We couldn't believe it.

As for what we came for, the festivities got underway the next day. First up were the elimination battles for the B-Boy and B-Girl title at the Marc Ballroom in Union Square. Miami crews Ground Zeroh and Street Masters sent representatives Legacy, Bebe, and Heps Fury to rock the floor and try to get the $1,000 prize money. To everyone's surprise but our own, Legacy from Ground Zeroh made it to the final round. Unfortunately, he lost to Gerald from Sacramento.

Disappointed in the outcome, but proud of the fact that one of our own made it to the final, we were in the process of dispersing when I ran into a personal hero, a direct inspiration for *The Cipher*, and a true legend in my eyes: the one and only Bobbito Garcia, aka The Barber, aka DJ Cucumber Slice, aka Kool Bob Love. World famous host of the WKCR 89tec9 FM radio show with partner DJ Stretch Armstrong, writer, author, documentarian, entrepreneur, etc. During my high school years, I read his monthly column in *Rap Pages* magazine without fail to catch up with the music and artists he championed.

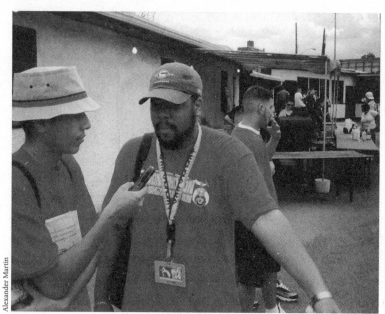

Interviewing Mr. Len of Company Flow
Rock Steady Crew's 21st Anniversary—NYC 1998

Interviewing DJ Rhettmatic of the Beat Junkies

By 1998, he founded and ran his independent record label Fondle 'Em Records, releasing The Juggaknots, MF Doom (RIP), The Arsonists, and other acts that I listened to. You know that saying "never meet your heroes?" Because if you do, you'll be disappointed? Nothing could be further from the truth. Bobbito set the tone for the rest of our stay up north. A real humble brother who opened up to some kid from Florida after spinning a set in the middle of the day in Manhattan. He defined the essence of Hip Hop: be creative, be original, and show respect to the foundation. He gave Miami props as well:

"I've been down to Miami. They got a good scene down there. It's always been small but it's always been strong. I went to a party out there back in '91, I think. Down the street from the Cameo Theater, it was like some real down low, fuckin graffiti on the wall, no bar, run down shit. There were kids up rockin and this kid Chris was spinnin like Poppa Large, Ultra, all this dope shit! And I was like wow, you know? You couldn't even hear Poppa Large in NY and I thought that shit was dope."

Still active after all these years, he has released three documentaries: "Doin' It In The Park" about the NYC streetball culture, "Stretch and Bobbito: Radio That Changed Lives" with his long time fellow legend DJ Stretch Armstrong, which covers the 89tec9 radio show that single handedly started the careers of countless rappers and luminaries throughout the 90's, and "Rock Rubber 45's" a biographical journey through his life and times.

After that high, we wandered the concrete jungle and then made it back to our backpacker hostel for some well-deserved rest.

The next day, as the rhymes from KRS rang in my head: "Now way back in the days when Hip Hop began/ with Coke La Rock, Kool Herc, and then Bam…" we took the 1 train to the place where it all started: The Bronx. Riding on the L, all I could see were the brick buildings and storefronts, nothing special. But the streets below were where hip hop culture first manifested in the early 70's. Finally, we arrived at our stop: 238th Street in Riverdale.

Gaelic Park was the spot for the live performances by The Arsonists, Dead Prez, Mos Def, Channel Live, Greg Nice, Heltah Skeltah, Black Moon, and Smif & Wessun. On the wheels of steel, Tony Touch and The 5th Platoon were holding it down, while Crazy Legs, Bobbito, and Ray Roll handled hosting duties. Summertime in the city means sweating your balls off, but we're from Miami so it's just another Saturday. The performances were all on point, as heads congregated from all sectors of the map. After chilling out for a bit, I had to get to work and just started interviewing random heads I found in the crowd: Mr. Len from Company Flow and DJ Rhettmatic of the Beat Junkies.

The park jam was all that and more, with the day capped off by an unforgettable radio appearance on WBAI 99.5 FM. A couple of heads we met at the Miami Pro-Am a few months prior hooked us up for a quick interview live on the air. Going out to the whole Tri-State was *The Cipher*, Miami's Hip Hop Newspaper in town for the 21st Rock Steady Crew anniversary. This was obviously the greatest visit to New York since King Kong's! We were crushing on all levels.

Still floating on cloud nine, we got dropped off at our hostel and, after giving much thanks to the homies, we jetted off into the night. Just two heads rollin' up and down the Village, taking in all the sights and sounds in the city that never sleeps. Of course I foolishly spent all my cash on vinyl and food (in that order) because who knows when I'll be back? The next day, Shareef and I spent all morning walking around Spanish Harlem trying to find an ATM that worked. Growing more and more heated as one after the other was either out of order or didn't have enough cash to dispense, it was all Shareef could do to contain himself.

We had to get back on the bus early Monday morning and I needed the cash in my hands like Greg Nice. After finally resolving that mess, we headed to the Manhattan Center in Midtown for the closeout performance. Arriving too late to see Common, we nevertheless beheld the RSC showcase turning into a real live battle as crews from all over the world called them out, and they went at them in their own spot!

For the closeout to this grand expedition, we headed to the world famous Roxy for the International Turntablist Federation DJ battle. Unfortunately, Shareef was underage and that meant no entry. I had to go solo for journalistic purposes while he took off to chill with other heads. Do I really need to tell you who won the turntablist competition? Of course not, because you already know DJ Craze did. As I headed back to the hostel, I reflected on the fact that while in the year 1998 the jiggy scene was king and hip hop was more commercial than ever, both young and old heads had gathered from all corners of the globe to participate and celebrate the culture, the talent, and the essence of hip hop where it was born. But now, it was time to head back to life, back to reality…

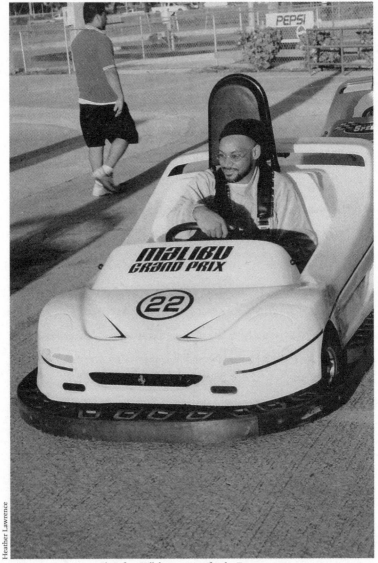

Ghostface Killah practicing for the Daytona 500

PART :3

INTERNAL AFFAIRS

Back in the 305, we got busy on the fifth issue. By now, the process was automatic: gather photos from events, pass off records and tapes to Shareef for review (by this point, I was too busy and burnt out to listen to records over and over in order to write a decent review), spread the gospel, collect checks and instructions from Cristina for advertisers, and politic on the scene for interviews and access.

Once all the content is typed up and printed, proceed to the cardboard for the layout, cutting and gluing paper, and then drive to Hialeah for the print run. Come back in a couple of days to stuff five thousand copies in bundles of three hundred, stuff the trunk and back seat, drive home, and from there, parcel them out to staff. Take some to The Point, Backway, Spec's, Uncle Sam's, Reggae Wear, Crazy Goods, Blue Note, Shoe Gallery, and any other store I could find. Staff and friends would distribute at their respective schools, and of course pass out copies at shows and club let outs. I remember getting heated when I would see copies strewn on sidewalks in South Beach. You know how hard we worked on this??? But what else could we do? We still weren't color, still on newsprint, and still free.

It was around this time that Crook and Crome from MSG achieved infamy in South Florida. Walls, trucks, freight trains, overpasses, rooftops, expressway signs, the heavens, no surface was safe from the spray cans wielded by the Miami Style Graffers.

By the late 90's, the amount of artistic vandalism was so serious that according to public radio station WLRN "Graffiti was a regular issue at commission meetings and town hall meetings. Graffiti on the highways prompted the Florida Department of Transportation to set aside a budget of over $130,000 to clean up tags on highway signs. There was also a hotline to report anyone seen doing graffiti."[****]

Meanwhile, every writer and head in town was amazed at the exploits of the dynamic duo who were fearless and winning the war against the buff. The *Miami New Times* reported: "Crook and Crome hit signs and walls along the highways harder than anybody had before. They made their straight-letters large and clear enough for civilians to decipher. Local news stations heaped them with publicity. When a WPLG-10 reporter kept referring to 'Crookcrome' as one person, Crome sent a lackey to the camera setup to whisper truth in the newsman's ear."[*****]

"We were spray painting everything from highway signs to curbs, and every little thing you could think of we were doing." Crome told 24hourhiphop.com.[******] "Some nights we would focus on Hialeah, the next night we would focus on Broward, and the next day it would be Palm Beach. Sometimes we would bust out a map and plan out our attack for the week so we could really cover a whole city. We would hit up all kinds of places and people realized that we were everywhere. We even went to Orlando on occasions.

**** Duba, Julia. "South Florida's Graffiti Problem In The '90s Had An Emblem: "Crook Crome"" WLRN, 16 Feb. 2015. wlrn.org/post/south-floridas-graffiti-problem-90s-had-emblem-crook-crome

***** Garcia-Roberts, Gus. "RIP, Ynot: MSG Cartel Mourns the Loss of a Graffiti Star." *Miami New Times*. 23 Sept. 2010. miaminewtimes.com/news/rip-ynot-msg-cartel-mourns-the-loss-of-a-graffiti-star-6379219

****** 24hourhiphop.com/features/honest-truth/automatic-attraction-the-story-behind-crome-miamis-infamous-graffiti-artist/

We definitely knew it was getting heated and that people were out to stop us."

What kind of people? On March 10th, 1999, Miami PD raided their apartment on Biscayne and 25th Street, where they arrested Crook without incident. "They say they're here to pick me up for attempted murder," he told Beyond Extreme magazine.******* "But if I tell them about this whole graffiti thing, they will get the charges dropped." Keep in mind that these are supposed to be Miami's finest. "I was amazed at how stupid these fuckin' pigs were. No search warrants, no case."

The whole spectacle was just for show. "Every fuckin' news station in Miami was there." He said. "Channel 4, 6, 7, 10, 33, 39, even the fuckin' Spanish channels." Crome, upon hearing of the raid and arrest, went into hiding, then to Atlanta, and finally turned himself in around six months later. He recalls: "I ended up staying with my friend in Broward for the night. As we were driving we drove by one of the walls that we had done and we saw the news crews in front of them. I realized that this shit was serious."

Clearly, this wasn't just another vandalism charge: "As soon as I got to my friend's crib in Broward I turned on the news and the main story was Crook. They showed him locked up. They were showing pictures of me on the television and they said that I was still on the loose but they expected to have me in custody by the end of the night."

Meanwhile, the Dade County D.A. asked for Crook's bail to be set at ONE MILLION DOLLARS! For graffiti! But Crome had

******* forum.12ozprophet.com/threads/crook-interview-from-miami-crook-crome.60201/

Heather Bee with Cam'Ron

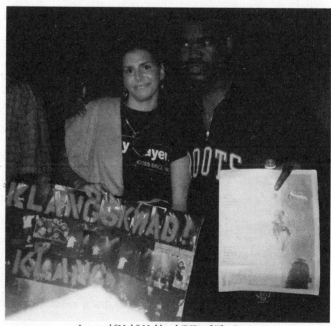

Leonard "Hub" Hubbard (RIP) of The Roots

OutKast in-store Tower Records NYC—1999

Hub representin' The Cipher

Graffiti case draws to an end

'Crook & Crome' charges dropped

BY MICHAEL GREENWALD
mgreenwald@herald.com

Prosecutors tried for 26 frustrating months to nail "Crook & Crome," the infamous, graffiti-painting duo who turned South Florida overpasses, interstate exit signs and buildings into their own personal canvas.

In a 30-second court appearance Friday, Miami-Dade Circuit Judge Roberto M. Piñeiro whitewashed everything — as the state dropped criminal mischief charges against ███████ ████████ and ███████ ████████.

In their heyday in early 1999, the work of "Crook & Crome" could be found scrawled all over Miami-Dade and Broward expressways and barren walls. The so-called "taggers" sometimes took daring risks, climbing on signposts and overpasses to leave their signatures high above the road.

Now, ███████ is a tattoo artist at Ace Tattoos in South Beach. He paints murals in his spare time. ███████ lives in Orlando and works at radio station 95live.com. He goes by the name "Crook" on his Saturday show, and doesn't paint much anymore.

CHARLES TRAINOR JR./HERALD STAFF

IT WASN'T ME: ███████ insists he had no role in a graffiti rampage. He painted this wall in Miami – legally.

"I'm definitely pleased that this case is finally over," ███████ said. Police identified him as "Crome," the more gifted of the two.

"I never did any of this graffiti," ███████ said. "And we're not 'Crook & Crome.'"

███████ was less firm in his denials.

"I'm not going to say I did it and I'm not going to say I didn't," he said. "If I was David Copperfield, would I really say how I made the Statue of Liberty disappear?"

Police insist they had the right guys.

"Since we arrested them, the graffiti has almost stopped," said Miami Police detective Antonio Hernandez, lead investigator on the case. "We had a mountain of evidence. And you just don't see 'Crook & Crome' written

▶ PLEASE SEE **GRAFFITI, 2B**

Duo deny they're notorious taggers

▶ GRAFFITI, FROM 1B

anywhere anymore."

That wasn't the case three years ago when the tags cropped up all over Miami and as far north as Disney World. Signs along Interstate 95 and State Road 836 were popular targets. So was a block-long abstract mural in the wholesale fashion district between Northwest 23rd and 24th streets beside I-95.

Tips led police to the duo's 275 NE 25th St. apartment on March 10, 1999. And there they found ███████ with spray paint cans, photo albums filled with pictures of graffiti — and even a videotape of the two admiring graffiti.

███████ obligingly drew his trademark "Crook" tag for police. "To my friends at ███████," he wrote.

But Judge Piñeiro threw out the evidence in April 2000, ruling that even though ███████ signed a written consent form authorizing the search, he did not do so freely.

"The police walked in on their own," said ███████ who wasn't home at the time.

"They just started doing whatever they wanted to do."

An appeals court upheld Piñeiro's ruling and the prosecution's case fell apart.

"I'm disappointed," Assis-

For two years, 'Crook & Crome' did their graffiti deeds all across South Florida

tant State Attorney Stephen Talpins said Friday. "But it does appear that tagging in Miami-Dade has diminished." Miami Police credit the publicity surrounding "Crook & Crome" with the decline and vow an aggressive crackdown if it happens again.

Though the duo's graffiti cost thousands of dollars to remove, their work drew mild praise from an unlikely source — the prosecuting attorney. "These guys have a lot of talent," Talpins said. "I just wish they directed their talents to a more constructive use."

███████, ever proclaiming his innocence, offered his own picture of the culprits. Just "some people trying to be infamous," he said with a slight smile.

"They never vandalized anyone's house or anyone's car. There were no victims to the crimes. I think they're fantastic people," other plans: "I ended up heading out to Atlanta to chill for a while and I heard that they tried giving Crook a million dollar bond. The judge said they were crazy and that he didn't even give kingpins, drug traffickers, or real criminals that kind of bond. The judge gave him a $50,000 bond and that was still too much. The prosecutors kept acting like we couldn't be controlled and that we were some kind of maniacs who were going to terrorize the streets if we were set loose. In reality we were just a couple of graffiti artists and everything was really overblown." In the end, Crook ended up serving seven months before his case was dismissed due to police raiding his apartment without a warrant. Crome also did a few weeks in lockup before charges against him were dropped due to illegal search and seizure.

However, the message was loud and clear: stop graffiti at all costs. And that's exactly what happened. Once writers and bombers saw that you could end up as the lead story on the 10 o'clock news with a million dollar bond over your head, illegal graffiti all but disappeared in South Florida. Within a couple of years following the Crook and Crome saga, all the big penits were demolished, the final nail in the coffin for Miami's golden age.

Nowadays, there's scattered tags and get ups throughout the city, and you can safely walk in Wynwood with police officers posted on every corner as you take pics with your smartphone (which you will not get jacked for) of block-long productions painted by top graffiti writers and muralists from around the globe, including Crook and Crome. But the days of free for all penits and nearly every available surface tagged, bombed, and pieced up are long gone.

As Crook says "Miami is a tourist town. Millions and millions of dollars come from people who don't live here. They come here for a few days…they do not want graffiti all over the place. Shows that they don't have control. I'll tell you one thing: Miami will never tolerate graffiti." That is, unless it's in the specially designated Wynwood Art District, where Art Basel pink pants wearing connoisseurs and hipsters on monthly art walks can patronize food trucks and Snapchat filter to death.

Now a free man, DJ Raw reflects on the turnaround of his old stomping grounds: "After the McDuffie riots and the Cano riots (in 1980 and 1990) most of that turf was burnt down and destroyed by us." He laments. "The mayor at that time came to see us and told us to stop burning down our own neighborhood, stop messing stuff up, and we did. But it was too late, we had ruined the neighborhood."

Both of the civic disturbances were a result of police brutality against Miami inner city residents. A few days before Christmas 1979, Arthur McDuffie, a black resident of Liberty City, was beaten to death by four white Miami police officers after a high-speed chase. The ensuing manslaughter trial was moved to Tampa, and the four officers were acquitted in May 1980, leading to several days of rioting in Miami's inner city. After the flames were doused, the final toll was eighteen dead and over $100 million in damages.

Nearly a decade later, Miami police officers once again went over the line, with fatal results. In December 1990, six white and Hispanic officers were acquitted on charges stemming from the beating that led to the death of Leonardo "Cano" Mercado, a street-level crack dealer in Wynwood. The ensuing rampage through

Miami's historically Puerto Rican neighborhood resulted in three million in damages.

Wynwood may have remained just another inner city ghetto if not for Tony Goldman and other developers who took a risk at the start of the new millennium. They invested in a neglected area where the authorities and others only saw drugs and crime. DJ Raw gives his viewpoint on gentrification: "I think that it's a plus, that they (the developers) came back and gave the opportunity for Hip Hop and for the graffiti artists to be able to embed themselves into the neighborhood and still give it that touch of class that it needs to sustain itself." But before them, he contributed to the artistic renaissance that brought galleries and nightclubs to formerly dope boy infested streets: "I paid most of the graffiti artists back at that time (mid-90's) to tag up, to bring that in. To see it evolve into where it is today? That's pretty amazing."

While Mayor Alex Penelas (of refusing to assist the federal government in the Elian Gonzalez case fame) and the Metro-Dade Police Department were putting the squeeze on the underground in the late 90's, the South Beach "rap industry" had mutated from its How Can I Be Down? experiment into a voracious monster swallowing everything in its path. With Hoodstock founder DJ Raw locked up, Peter Thomas and Jimmy Henchmen relocated their spectacle to Montego Bay after one too many roadblocks from Miami Beach City Hall. In their wake, the Mixshow Power Summit moved in. Geared towards radio personalities and jocks, it was a bit more subdued (meaning no shootouts.) I appreciated the fact that we were getting to see more shows, but in the end it was more of

Lil' Kim album release party—Miami 1999

the same: industry heads flying down, getting put up at a hotel on the beach, and completely ignoring the local scene. Mic Rippa? DJ Snowhite? B-Boy crews? No love whatsoever.

The only ones who had broken out were DJ Craze, who was completely dominating the DJ battle arena, and DJ Infamous, his fellow Allies turntablist crew member. Nowadays he's a Grammy-winning producer for Lil' Wayne, Yo Gotti, Fat Joe, and many others, but back then Inf was wrecking turntables and getting props on the DJ circuit. Everyone else? Just open up the show and then get out. Here's what I wrote after I went to the opening night of the 1998 MPS:

> Ask yourself this question: Do you ever feel like saying "fuck Hip Hop!" and moving on to some other shit? Not me. After this wonderful evening with all kinds of ghetto superstars, I am more determined to represent and keep it real at all costs. No doubt, my Big Willie experience was enhanced by the fact that I was able to actually be in the same room as the Sporty Thievz, John Forte, DJ Skribble, Jazzy Joyce, Red Alert, Dr. Dre, Tony Touch, Black Rob, and Ski from Rok-a-Blok.

> See, usually I support the underground movement, but after seeing the benefits of blowing up (complimentary Dom P, lap dances, groupies, etc.) I feel like investing in an iced-down medallion. Various industry reps were in the house, so I took full advantage of the situation: "yo man, check out *The Cipher*," I would say. "Word life kid, you gotta put my artist up in this piece, dunn." At this point, cards and

pounds were exchanged. "Be sure to send a stack of promos and VIP passes to your next function" was my sign-off.

Making my way through the packed-like-sardines crowd, I see people getting jiggy with it and flossing hard. How desperately I wanted to join in the unrestrained orgy of affluence! DJ Skribble was cutting "Money Ain't a Thing," the bar was raking in the dough, and the chickenheads were just getting warmed up. Now it's the stars' time to shine. First up, John Forte kicking some cuts from his album and then exiting with a positive speech, something about "the children are the future." Don't nobody wanna hear that shit tonight, so chill.

By this time, I'm high off the contact and ready to call it a night, but Ski's monologue persuaded me to stick around and bear witness to his producing greatness. As the DJ cued up "Luchini," he let everybody within a twenty-mile radius know that he produced it. Stuck off the realness, I stood glued to my spot as "Who You With?" boomed over the speakers. "I did it! Ski from Rok-a-Blok nigga!!" My mouth fell to the floor in utter amazement. Finally! My life is almost complete. I had become converted to the ways of the Big Willie. Next up, Sporty Thievz. Hey, I wanna wear Hawaiian shirts and prance around stages too.

The night ended with me achieving nirvana and experiencing a revelation that will remain unequaled for as long as I walk the earth: I felt possessed by the thug essence as Noreaga's 'Superthug' was pumping loud and my eyes

Black Eyed Peas

Destiny's Child backstage at Wyclef's Carnival—Miami 1999

fell upon a hoodrat lifting her very brief miniskirt as the hook kicked in. What. What!! I had to see this up close. Waving my Washingtons in the air, I proceeded to get a free show and props from those in attendance. It has all been decided: I am now trading in my Adidas for a Versace suit. Watch me now!

This was an average night at any club in South Beach. The fact that this particular party took place at Club Liquid (now a tourist t-shirt store), which was partially owned by mobbed up impresario Chris Paciello, fit in perfectly with the narrative of commercial hip hop. As '98 was winding down, I was already beginning to burn out from the late nights, the politics, and the stress. But I didn't choose the nightlife. The nightlife chose me, so it was on to the next. Thankfully, Sunz of Man came down to perform on a promo run at Studio 183 in Miami Gardens, which had hosted raves, comedy nights, and hood rap shows for years. It was a bittersweet welcome relief from the commercial beach scene, as I noted in our sixth issue:

"The dressing room backstage at Studio 183. A somber Phife Dawg takes a seat as Godfree and I gather around and set up the tape recorder. No small talk is exchanged, for what we have just heard has left us speechless: A Tribe Called Quest is no more. After five albums and three classics in a row, the group that carried the torch for innovation and creativity throughout the 90's is calling it quits." Naturally, we all wanted to know why. Also on my mind was the fact that we were scooping the rest of the media—all the big national rags had lead times of at least a couple of months, which meant that we would be getting the exclusive and out on the streets first. Although we had nowhere near the reach of *The Source* or *Rap Pages*, at least we had South Florida covered, and that was what we were all about to begin with. I suppose it was only fitting that our biggest story ever appeared in the God seventh issue:

Growing up listening to ATCQ, the thought never ever crossed my mind that they were capable of separating and pursuing different paths; it's almost like the natural order of the universe has been altered. Imagine the sun not rising tomorrow: that's the feeling I get knowing that Q-Tip, Phife, and Ali are no more. Goddamn! Was it only yesterday that I was losing my mind at a house party when the DJ spun "Scenario" or kicking game to a honey as "Electric Relaxation" played in the background? The early 90's without Tribe would be like the late 80's without Eric B. & Rakim or the mid-70's without Kool Herc. Trendsetters and innovators are generally not acknowledged until their time has passed, but Tribe got love from the get-go.

While "Bonita Applebum" caught on with the pop crowd, any true head can recite "Luck of Lucien" off the top of their head. Their ability to crossover yet not sell out or switch styles remains unmatched. Able to rock Lollapalooza and The Apollo at the same time, Quest seemed simple and to the point on the surface. True, they never had super-complex scientifical rhymes or way out samples, but the secret to their success remained in making the difficult seem easy: Three back to back to back classic albums, never

Showing love to The Cipher

rhyming about the same thing twice, and working with everyone from Ron Carter to Busta Rhymes.

It's not every day that I get to build with someone whose voice accompanied me from middle school to my first year of college; it felt like meeting a long-lost friend or relative. However, nothing could be worse than talking about breaking up and moving on. Originally scheduled for an autograph session at Spec's South Beach and a show at Studio 183, Tip and Ali couldn't make it out of New York, leaving the Phifer on a solo mission. Having arrived on the late night flight from Atlanta, where he currently resides, he was visibly tired. Rocking a matching Mets cap and jersey with mint-condition Nike Airs, he spoke at length about the past, present, and future. To some of the new jacks this might seem a little over-dramatic, but Hip Hop will never be the same.

Omen: What was the reason for the break up?

Phife: It's no internal beef or nothing like that, we've been doing it for ten years as far as y'all know, but it's really like twenty years for us. We felt like we said everything we could say as A Tribe Called Quest. I guess maybe it's a point where we've outgrown each other to a certain extent. Tip's gonna do an album, I'm gonna do an album. We still keeping it in the family, just not under that name.

As far as the break up, we still down, but we'll take different avenues to success and just handle our business. Maybe

Hip Hop bedrooms

Saafir backstage at Club Cream—Miami 1998

What is Timbaland looking at here?—Backstage at Wyclef's Carnival—Miami 1999

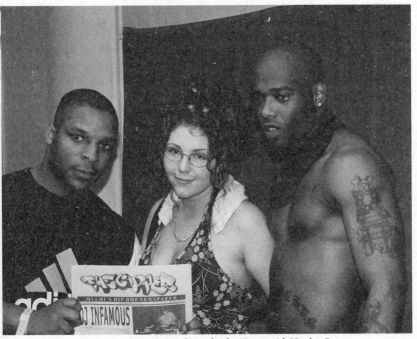

Vinnie (L) and Treach (R) of Naughty by Nature with Heather Bee
backstage at Wyclef's Carnival—Miami 1999

later on in the future we'll come back together as a team, but right now it's a dead issue. Making records for Jive is like in vain as far as I'm concerned, cuz they're not putting their full foot in it to make it go anywhere. KRS-One's barely going gold! It has more to do with business than internal beef. Every group has problems but we've always been able to squash our differences. It's just time to move on and try other things.

Omen: What are your most memorable experiences from the years?

Phife: Damn, it's a lot of those. As far as recording, doing "Scenario" with Leaders. Cuz little [does] everybody know, we did like five different versions. At one point, it was us, Leaders, Black Sheep, our manager Chris Lighty was even rhyming on it. It's like a whole bunch of different "Scenarios" we did. Pos from De La was on it. As far as touring, Lollapalooza 94 was an ill experience. Cuz I ain't really wanna go, but at the end of the day it was a fat check!

The highlight of my career was moving out of New York to Atlanta. Getting my own crib, no parents, just down south chillin. As far as performing, I don't know...Lollapalooza was cool, but one of our best shows was probably at Norfolk State University back in '91 when Low End [had] just come out. Cuz the way people accepted us, that was kind of a shock. We never got into it knowing we'd be accepted like that, we just did it cuz we loved doing it. At Howard homecoming, that was like the illest show: people bumrushing the stage, girls faking like they was gonna faint just to get up on stage and touch us, that shit was crazy!

Omen: What do you feel has been the legacy ATCQ left for Hip Hop? Some people talk about People's Travels and Low End as blueprints for Hip Hop albums. Does that make you look back as trendsetters?

Phife: I don't like to pat myself on the back but if there was a Hip Hop hall of fame I think we'd be up in there. We were always in our own little world. If it was a Mobb Deep, Noreaga, or Jay-Z that came out, we stayed in our little spot and did what we had to do as artists. I don't think we really were that different, it was just so many people being the same. A lot of people duplicating each other's rhyme styles, cadences, beats. There was a time in Hip Hop where you'd get your shit smacked if you bite the next man's beat or if you bit his cadence.

Backstage at Studio 183 with Phife of A Tribe Called Quest
who had just announced their break-up

As far as Low End, People's, and Midnight being emulated, we couldn't even emulate it in a way. That stuff was a curse for us because look what happened on Beats, Rhymes, and Life. Niggas was like "What the hell is that?" There comes a time [where] you gonna have high points [and] low points. But one point we always had was that we was consistent. Hence the reason why I always tell people that EPMD was one of my favorite groups, because they maintained that gold status. I'm happy for what we accomplished, hopefully brothers and sisters that come out now like Lauryn, Erykah Badu, Outkast, Goodie Mob . . . I respect them cuz they being themselves.

When you look at all the albums that we've come out with, they always had a meaning to it. "People's Instinctive Travels and The Paths of Rhythm," a lot of people can't even adjust to what that means. It's saying that people have the instinct to travel. Anywhere you go, take the train, bus, car; you got a tape deck, boombox, got your music. People have an instinct to travel in the paths of rhythm; music makes the world go round. "The Low End Theory," our meaning is: the black man, or Latino, us basically, are always at the low end of the totem pole no matter how you look at it. And then the other meaning is the bass that we had within that album, cuz it was strictly boom boom boom! "Midnight Marauders," to maraud is to steal, loot. We was trying to steal y'all attention, your eardrums. The midnight part, everything we did was at night. We party at night, fuck girls at night (laughter), hit the studio at midnight.

"Beats, Rhymes, and Life," that's self-explanatory. "The Love Movement," everybody's talking about their love for chicks, cars, gold, platinum, jewels, and all of that. Our love is the love for the music, the love that we got for mankind, for our family. We need to get back to that cuz it's not a lot of people talking about love for your family. Once you have all the success, shining lights, red carpet rolled down for you, you gotta give thanks to Allah and your family for being there and supporting you. We trying to reach out to the youngsters hoping that they can get up on it. But like I said, they into the cars and Glocks. You can't really beat it right now, you just gotta let 'em know that there's something else they can latch on to.

ATCQ did eventually reunite for the Rock The Bells tour in 2007. In the meantime, the members enjoyed varying degrees of solo success, with Q-Tip scoring a club hit with "Vivrant Thing." Phife's solo was released to mixed reviews, while Ali Shaheed Muhammad branched off into Lucy Pearl in collaboration with Dawn from En Vogue, who of course Phife used to have a crush on, and The Midnight Hour with Adrian Younge. The "Beats, Rhymes, and Life" documentary by Michael Rappaport laid bare their struggles and conflicts, with ugly scenes to boot. In 2016, they released "We Got It From Here…Thank You For Your Service" a brilliant grown man rap album blessed with rhymes from the Phifer before he tragically passed on March 22, 2016 due to complications from diabetes.

Now that the five-foot freak is resting in peace while Ali and the brother abstract pursue solo careers, it remains to be seen

Gettin' busy at the Crazy Goods store

whether they can capture the magic of summer '92 when "Scenario" became a hip hop classic. In the immortal words of Phife Dawg: "When's the last time you heard a funky diabetic?"

As 1998 came to a close in Dade County, one collective stood out among the rest with their grind, hustle, and non-stop work ethic: Crazy Hood Productions. As supporters and sponsors of *The Cipher* since day one, it was only right that a long-overdue profile of those crazy-ass Kendall kids finally made it to print:

Driving westbound on Kendall Drive, my field of vision is bombarded with bright yellow snipes proclaiming the arrival of "Miami's Mix Tape King." Making a right on Southwest 107th Avenue, I notice that "Da Alliance" are "Coming Soon." Who are these people and what do they want from me? Besides taking up every inch of available space, they also have the Crazy Goods store over by Braddock High School, a clothing line, website, mixtapes, and a team of MCs. I caught up with Crazy Hood Productions after they opened for Sunz of Man at Studio 183 and managed to get the scoop.

DJ EFN heads up this highly organized unit, with Da Alliance coming out on the rhyme tip. MCs Heckler and Weird Thoughts first met at Sunset High School and after deciding that it would be more beneficial to unite their separate crews under one banner, they got with CHP and thus Da Alliance was born, with Gambit joining soon after. Their first effort, "Fake Outta Towners" between "Live and Uncut," kicked up a storm of controversy that still rages to this day. Thoughts explain the reasoning behind that particular record: "We all had thought the same shit, like, wassup with this fake cat here, there's a fake club there… we got mad heat up for that cuz niggas was like 'oh, y'all dissing everybody from out of town.' But if they heard what we said, it wasn't like that."

EFN remembers going to clubs back in '92 such as "The Zoo" where, according to him, "it was New York to the fullest." He goes on to explain "that's cool and everything because New York is the birthplace of Hip Hop. But you can only rep another place so far till it gets to a ridiculous point when we're in Miami and you don't even hear a word about Miami. We'll take that to a certain extent cuz that was '92, so OK, maybe these cats just got here so they're still from New York. But '93, '94, '95…you been here for a minute already. Then they flip it on each borough, so then they reppin the boroughs to the fullest. It got to the point when we were saying 'None of us are originally from Miami… but we live here, been living here over five years.' If you've been here over a month, you're living here, paying your bills here. We are Miami residents so we represent Miami.

It was shocking to hear someone address what I like to call the "How Can I Be Down" syndrome. Symptoms include: an overwhelming desire to pretend one is from New York even though one has never been there, moving down here from New York and still acting like the local area code is 212 or 718, and saying over and over "Miami's wack, I wish I was back in NY." EFN has little

dead prez and crew backstage at The Cameo—Miami 1998

Tino interviewing Andre 3000 of OutKast backstage at The Cameo—Miami 1999

tolerance for such people: "Fake Outta Towners has a lot of different reasons," he says. "It could be a person coming from New York and just cold disrespecting Miami. If he comes saying Miami's wack and disrespects everybody here, that's a fake outta towner. If you live here and you don't get it in your mind 'I live here, let me rep here, do my best for the Hip Hop community here' then you're a fake outta towner."

Owing largely to a low-budget environment, EFN humbles himself: "It wasn't one of the best tracks we've done, we don't even say that. That was one of the first tracks we've done." However, the message overrode any reservations he might've had. "We think that finally people are gonna appreciate someone saying this, so let's put it on wax. We knew it wasn't nothing special. Put it out, what happened? The fake outta towners went crazy! If your emotions were touched then you knew what we was talking about. Cuz if you got hurt by the track, then the song was for you." Gambit recalls a specific instance where "We did a show, had about 20 New Yorkers up front talking about 'fuck you, fuck you!' the funny shit was that five months later, we played a jam and everybody was showing love like 'word, we finally heard ya'll niggas.' Ya'll muthafuckas wake the fuck up!"

At the same time, Weird Thoughts questions the integrity of certain figures in the Miami scene. "Some DJs is funny," he begins. "When we in the club, they be 'Where Brooklyn at?' then they see EFN or us and all of a sudden, it's 'Where's Hialeah and Kendall at?' If you gonna do one way, do one way." EFN also heard rumors of shady business tactics: "important Hip Hop figures in our community got really touched by the song, didn't wanna play it, banned it on their own, and caught beef with us because of it. Those same people are coming back at us now talking about 'lace a track for us, do a dubplate for me.' It's hilarious!"

However, it's not all about calling move-fakers out on wax—Crazy Hood Productions operates with a very serious business mentality. EFN set it off in 93 with his mixtapes. "I'm the only person that I know of that came out with a mixtape reppin Kendall," he says.

There might've been somebody else, I'm not downing nobody else. Everybody that we know was like "Why would you wanna rep Kendall? Kendall's like a suburb. Rep Perrine, Perrine's ghetto." I live in Kendall. What the fuck, I'm not gonna rep where I'm living? We did tapes called "Live From Kendall Drive," "Still Live From Kendall Drive," "Attack From Kendall Sector." The first tape we did with Heckler was called "The Double 8," meaning 88th St. The desired effect is to duplicate what happened in New York during the 80's. Each borough would battle towards each other. Cats in The Bronx is like, "we the best." Niggas in Queens are like "fuck that, we the best." I figured we can start that chain reaction here in Miami; we represent Kendall to the fullest. Somebody in Hialeah could be like "fuck them niggas in Kendall, we gonna rep." Coral Gables, Homestead, and so on. In the end, it's all gonna be love, cuz if we keep it on wax and tapes, then at the end we have a stronger Hip Hop

community. We wasn't trying to be rowdy Kendall niggas,
we just want it to escalate to all these other communities.

In the years since this interview took place, CHP has enjoyed increased success and diversified even more. Gambit morphed into Garcia, releasing albums and collaborating with Noreaga. EFN jumped behind the scenes to co-manage Mayday! and released "Another Time" in 2016, a critically acclaimed all-star compilation. They have also produced, filmed, and released the "Coming Home" documentary series, in which they have traveled to Cuba, Peru, Haiti, Vietnam, and Colombia to showcase the homegrown hip hop scenes there, and picked up a couple of festival accolades along the way. By far, the biggest splash has been the "Drink Champs" podcast, hosted by EFN and Noreaga, which has provided classic episodes with Nas, 50 Cent, Fat Joe, and many more. It is at the top of the download charts, having inked a deal with Mass Appeal (Nas), Tidal (Jay-Z), and Revolt TV (Puff). Still grinding, they have never given up or slacked on their mission, coming Straight Outta Kendall.

One aspect of the scene that was also blowing up in the late 90s was the street promotion hustle. As the major labels took note of Miami becoming a big market for hip hop, they invested large sums into the hand-to-hand street teams popularized by Steve Rifkind at Loud Records. From the simple days of club flyers, it wasn't long before the beach was littered with stickers, banners, t-shirts, snipes, wheat pasting, and enough paper to make the most hardened environmentalist red with rage.

Off The Hook (Juan Galan and Edwin), Phatman Promotions (Fresh and Big Will), 360 (Mira and A.D.), On Point

Slick Rick

Ghostface Killah

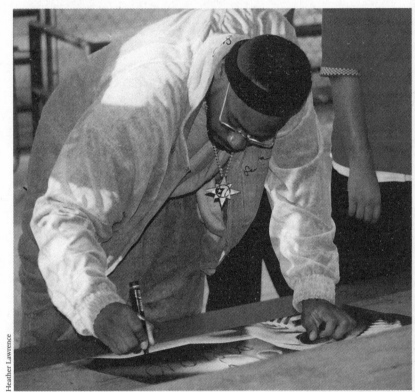

Ghostface Killah

(Boogah and Arthur), Public Wizard (Semp Rok), and Street Dwellaz (Alfonso and Dekwan) had the major label accounts. We built relationships ('lots and lots of polys!' as my guy Serge would say) with all of them, but got tight with Off The Hook. Juan explains how the street promotion game worked: "Our hustle was to break artists in the market. Strip clubs, college radio, the pirates, anywhere we could get records played." Getting the major label accounts was based on reputation, networking, word of mouth, and referrals. "Having an account was like having money," he said. "Somebody from the label might call people in Miami that he knows, and ask them who's the dopest street team out there. They'll give you a call and put you on to work their stuff. Product was gold: vinyl, snippets, tapes, CDs, shirts, stickers."

By the end of the 90's, the street promoters had the city on lockdown. No wall, light post, sidewalk, club let-out, windshield, and hand was safe from the flyers, posters, snipes, and stickers handed out by kids wanting to get put on, including us. One night, Godfree and I got a promo package from Mira for the J.Lo and George Clooney "Out of Sight" movie. So we drove all night from Carol City to Westchester, wheat pasting on the expressway underpasses and walls around movie theaters, risking arrest or a beatdown only to get paid with an advance screening ticket. But that was the game, and it was fun for us. On another occasion, Fresh put us on the DMX/Onyx campaign, for which we stapled snipes by high school entrances, causing kids to rip them down and parade them at school the next day.

Heather Lawrence

will.i.am of the Black Eyed Peas with fans—
Wyclef's Carnival Miami 1999

We never caught beef like the other crews, but check out this little tidbit from Juan: "We was out at Club Onyx, putting our stickers [for Cam'Ron and Charli Baltimore] and Fat Joe and them came outside. We just got into a real heated argument with them. They were taking our stickers down, we were taking theirs down… we used to do that stuff cuz it was hard to get positioning. The labels made us compete, because everybody wanted their stuff in the prime locations." The race for advertising real estate led to drama between the street teams, as well as sacrificing personal lives and academic careers. Sound familiar? "You had to get up early, 2-3 in the morning to go put up these posters and pray that by the morning time, they'd still be there." And it wasn't all fun and games either. "We got fined, locked up. There were consequences."

But they weren't limited to just music. They also expanded to what he called the lifestyle accounts "like Flava Station, Shoe Gallery, [and] Reggae Wear." There were also the promo vinyl handouts every Wednesday night on 6th and Washington in front of Club Cream where DJs and record junkies gathered to receive stacks of free records from label reps. Maybe all this unrestrained spending had something to do with the industry's demise post-Napster? Naaah, it's easier to blame technology. But the Internet and MP3s did kill the street promotion hustle. "We went from physically handing DJ's vinyl and CD's to the labels to sending MP3s." Just like factories being relocated to China, the street promoters were downsized to cut costs. Anyway, we soon got in on the act, and even though most street teamers got paid with t-shirts and advance music, that was good enough for me at first.

In hindsight, there was definitely a conflict of interest in promoting Rawkus and major label artists on the beach and then editing a publication that wrote about them. At the time however, no one was paying us, and I highly doubt Def Jam's marketing department even knew we existed. Nevertheless, I was aware of the need to keep the street promotion separate from the publication. This was made crystal clear when Lenny Moore, an ex-Miami Hurricanes linebacker who had invited me to his office to inquire about writing for his Black Gold "adult hip hop magazine" turned around and then shamelessly published our artwork in his first issue without so much as a "thank you."

This was an outright theft, but they were glossy, full color, with investors, aka everything we were not. So of course we got jacked and couldn't do shit about it, since we were not incorporated and were distributed freely. As soon as it happened, I let the rest of the team know that we had to incorporate as a company and have some kind of legal standing. Heather did the advance work and told us it was pretty straightforward: for less than $100 we could incorporate in the State of Florida and divide our ownership shares three ways: Cristina, Heather, and myself. We filed the papers, incorporating as Cipher Enterprises and kept to our schedule, our scene, and our love for the culture.

The highlight of the last quarter of '98 was the Lyricist Lounge tour stop at the Cameo Theater on October 24th. NFA promoted the hell out of it and the joint was packed as dead prez, Saafir, Common, Talib Kweli, and De La Soul with surprise guest Q-Tip rocked the crowd. Finally some artists I was actually into came to South Beach! In the meantime, Mic Rippa was busy winning rap battles and, by this point, rivals weren't even trying anymore. On the B-Boy tip, battles were going strong inside the clubs now, something unthinkable just a couple of years prior. Even *Blaze* magazine got into the act, sponsoring a showdown at Club Zen where Crazy Legs was one of the judges.

Personally, I had devoted all my energy to *The Cipher* with everything else on the backburner. I was dealing with girls left and right in Dade and Broward, still at Spec's collecting checks and props, and partying/working about four nights a week on average. On top of that, relations within the staff were fraying. Mostly, it had to do with my personality as a procrastinator and a perfectionist, a bad combination.

Since we had sponsors paying us, I wanted to make sure we had a good product out on time, and would crack the whip on the writers, illustrators, and Cristina to get me their output ASAP so I could print, cut, and paste it for the printing plant. Of course, nobody likes to be made to feel inept, especially when working for free. This led to the inevitable sarcastic and passive-aggressive behavior of not answering calls, returning calls when we felt like it, ignoring deadlines... things of that nature. We were all acting like children while trying to run a business. Of course, it all came to a head by the time the eighth and ninth issues dropped.

The cover for the eighth issue was of a kid at the RSC park jam with an airbrushed jumpsuit. It was a cute pic, but when blown up, it was pixelated and distorted. On top of that, the font and header for *The Cipher* looked horrendous. But it was too late, we simply

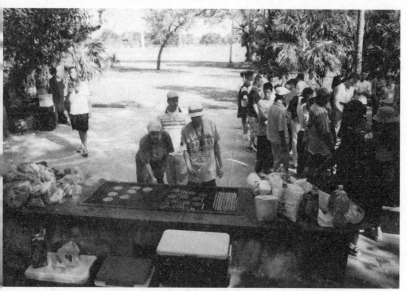

Live at the BBQ with RME crew

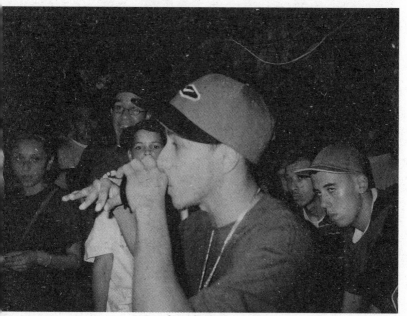

B Dope freestyling—Miami 1999

had to get it to the printer. The ninth issue was even worse in my opinion. We had Big Boi from Outkast holding a copy of the sixth issue, which was great, but the header was a graffiti style done by Renegade, leaving no consistency with the previous issues. In fact, we barely used our formal logo. I mean we had business cards and press passes, but the dripping graf logo looked wack on them. It was time to make a change, and that's when shit hit the fan.

I was extremely burnt out, tired, and sick of all the drama. The petty fights, politics of the scene, and pressure to top the last issue had taken its toll. In a huff, I felt I couldn't work with Cristina anymore. Once you get to non-speaking terms, what's the use? My personal life was also in shambles: failing classes at FIU, having to find a place to live after my mom decided to move back to Orlando (no way I was going back, especially now that the paper was in effect), and my 1990 Honda Civic hooptie giving me fits. Greeting 1999 (Year of the Ruff Ryders) with a head full of drama, I decided enough was enough and broke out. Composing my resignation email after yet another fight, I wrote, "I, John Cordero, officially resign as senior editor of The Cipher- Miami's Hip Hop newspaper and release my 33% ownership in shares of stock of Cipher Enterprises, Inc." Done.

However, it wasn't that simple. On the one hand, I hated to let my baby go, but I had to. On the other, who would take ownership of my shares? My first thought was Shareef, but he was also busy with school and while he was a staff member, I wasn't 100% sure. In the end, I decided to hold on to them for the time being while I planned and got my living situation sorted out. Long past niceties, I wrote another email: "I made a mistake in my letter,

I didn't specify who was taking my stock so I will hold on to it... basically, I am resigning as editor but still keeping my shares in Cipher Enterprises." By this point, it was too much for Cristina, who also resigned very publicly, publishing an editorial in the ninth issue laying bare all her frustrations and disappointment with the scene and the paper. I didn't see it until it was printed, and of course some took sides, others thought we were finished. For me, it lit a fire, motivating me to show and prove that we weren't going away. The fact that Gang Starr, one of my all-time favorites, was performing soon was the spark I needed:

> Usually, I avoid driving anywhere outside Dade County. The endless farmland, trees, and isolation provoke manic-depressive states in my mental. However, once word got down that Gang Starr would be performing at Club Boca, I had to find a companion who would undertake the hour-long drive with me to Palm Beach County. Securing the necessary transportation and crew, we headed out on the night of December 21st, 1998, and witnessed one of the greatest all-time classic shows ever.

> Guru showed up in mack-milli mode, rocking an all leather outfit and heading straight for the VIP area. Primo was absent due to studio commitments with the rapper formerly known as Nasty Nas. However, this would not prevent the Gifted, Unlimited...fuck the rest, ya'll niggas know him, from delivering a super charged performance. Opening up was Lil Dap of the Group Home, setting it off right and exact with "Supa Star" and "Livin' Proof." Giving

a shout out to his homie Melachi locked up in prison, Guru stepped in the arena as the filled to capacity venue loudly approved of his presence. For the next hour, it was vintage Gang Starr in the form of "Take It Personal," "Code of The Streets," "I'm The Man," "Step In The Arena," and "The Militia." Also, bonus freestyles and words of wisdom were imparted. Overall, a timeless show and one for the history books.

But now comes the fun part for me. Wanna get a rapper vexed? Just follow these simple instructions: Let him or her know that you are from a magazine and wish to conduct an interview. Immediately, you will be counted amongst the damned and targeted for destruction. It's not enough that you suffer, but your publication must perish also. Publicists and label reps attempt in vain to arrange sit downs, but MCs insist on showing up late and/or blunted. In their eyes, the media is the enemy, and we must be avoided and eliminated at all costs.

Oh wait, wrong magazine. The Cipher has never encountered these kinds of problems. That is, until Gang Starr's Guru made an appearance at the now-defunct Club Boca. Now, the rules of engagement dictate that one is to never approach a rapper when said subject is in the VIP area and conversing with a female. But then again, rules were made to be broken, right? Not only am I brave enough to interrupt Guru's mack session, but then I have the audacity of requesting an interview on the heels of a new jack magazine's "Top 50 MCs" issue, from which the Baldhead Slick was inexplicably absent. Needless to say, I am treated like a mere peasant and banished from the exclusive club area.

"I ain't talking to no media," is the announcement from the one Keith Elam. "Cuz [they] came out with that 50 MCs and didn't put me in it." As his entourage begins to make their way to the stage, I calmly explain that The Cipher is not to be compared with other corporate created publications. "I don't give a fuck!" he yells. Undaunted, I position myself next to the walking mountain aka bouncer and decide to wait until after the show, with visions of Puff Daddy running up in my office with champagne bottles filling my head.

A fun-filled hour later, we make our way to the club's offices. The only thing I wanna know is why does he hate the media so? His answer comes fast and forceful, and I wonder if I have made a mistake. "They killed Biggie, Pac, and continuously promote propaganda." At least he has a good point there, so I ask him to elaborate. "[It's] affecting the personal lives of rappers that ain't even supposed to be in the public [eye]." The often hazy boundary between the public's right to know and a popular figure's private life is often crossed, but in Hip Hop the added weight of rumors and gossip often lead to a volatile mix.

Guru's take on the situation leads to an all-out assault on self-appointed critics. "So-called Hip Hop media?" he asks.

Guru (RIP) of GangStarr performing in Miami—1999

"Some of them, they good in spurts, and in other spurts, they be fucking up! For the simple fact that, fuck your opinion! You ain't from the streets and you ain't from the culture, so what the fuck you got an opinion for? Just sit back and watch!"

It is now time to shift gears before the interview comes to an abrupt halt. Full Clip: 10 Years of Gang Starr is a testament to their legendary status. Who would have thought that a shady contract with Wild Pitch Records would lead to global acclaim and a firm reputation as one of Hip Hop's champions? Not to mention DJ Premier's status as the dominant force in music production. "One thing about me and him is that he can experiment with me," exclaims the Ill Kid. "All the other rappers come to him because of the original Gang Starr sound. They might have commercial shit on their albums, but when they get a Premier track, they ain't getting no commercial shit." The close bond that these two have developed over the past decade transcends just the music, according to Guru. "I'm proud of him. When he puts his signature on a beat, I feel like I'm there. I love him and ain't nothing gonna happen to him as long as I'm around."

The one word that sums up the Gang Starr experience is essence. Capturing it and putting it on wax has been their daily operation since day one. The last time you heard a wack Gang Starr track was never, so it should come as no surprise that Guru finds solace in music from

More Hip Hop bedrooms

Honest Benevolent stressed over the layout

Backstage with Canibus The Temple—1999 Miami

The Cipher staff backstage with Black Thought of The Roots

all the personal problems that have plagued him for the last two years. "'97 was a real bad year" is his summary of the allegations that swirled around him. "So then '98 was kinda like Allah blessed me, cuz '97 was like going through hell." Their fifth LP, Moment of Truth, became that odd rarity in Hip Hop, achieving both critical praise and commercial success.

Regarding the negative energy that he received in '97, Guru gives up his earlier animosity and calmly recounts how "they tried to hold a good brother down. They still trying to do it, they always underrate us. I suppose if I rhyme every song about sex, guns, and stuff. I talk about stuff like that, but I talk about it in a way where there's a lesson. That's why they call me Guru." The wise sage from Brooklyn by way of Boston acknowledges the power of karma: "I gotta be happy with what I got. It's like that saying: be careful what you pray for, you just might get it."

The love Guru and Group Home got at this particular show does not go unnoticed, even if he has been rocking stages for ten years. "This crowd was dope," he admits. "It was mad fun, I busted mad sweats. That's the best part of the whole shit, cuz a night like tonight will make me forget about whipping somebody's ass at that magazine. I ain't gonna say no names." Hey, I can keep a secret if you can.

Club Boca was an anomaly: located in a strip mall a good hour away from party central South Beach, they somehow always managed to bring down top-tier acts. Heather was always bugging me to go, but

I really didn't want to have to drive that far and worse yet, drive back late at night. But this night was well worth it. Who knew that Gang Starr would break up, that Guru would pass away? I give thanks that I got to see him perform when I had the chance, just like Big Pun and Phife Dawg (RIP).

This and the Phife interview were my personal highlights thus far. Yes, I was feeling myself for turning what could have been a total wreck into a manageable story with another one of my heroes, an MC I had been listening to since the eighth grade. Needless to say, his passing on April 19th, 2010 was devastating, a major loss for hip hop.

For the new year 1-9-9-9, we led off with a Dungeon Family feature, having interviewed Outkast, Cool Breeze, and Witchdoctor before they performed at the Cameo on Super Bowl weekend, where the Denver Broncos defeated the Atlanta Falcons at Joe Robbie Stadium (I don't care what it's called now, it will always be Joe Robbie Stadium to me).

The night of the performance, we rolled to yet another night on the beach. Stashing my hooptie at my usual spot where there's always parking (still exists, if you don't know by now...), we arrive at Cameo's side door and announce to security that we're from *The Cipher*. "You good, just go on up." What? No drama? No frontin'? We geek out on some "yo, we large!" This wasn't no local flavor, this was a LaFace Records showcase/Dirty South homecoming/Super Bowl celebration. Going up the stairs, I thought we had finally made it. Turns out the ATL also had its own local hip hop publication, *The Cypher,* a fact we found out later on that night. Great minds...

That night, it looked like Outkast would stay together forever, but we all know what happened. I also felt that *The Cipher* staff would remain committed for the long haul as the paper continued to grow and expand, getting bigger and better. But it was not to be. However, in the tenth issue, we finally got over the design and layout obstacle. Honest went to work and produced an amazing layout. I was proud to finally have an image that matched our content. In 1999, we were coming for the crown!

And what do you know, we came up on our first anniversary. I couldn't believe it. After all the fights, drama, and burnout, we made it! But, of course, we had also changed in a major way. Gone were the days of covering independent, underground, and unknown artists. We now had regular major label coverage, were welcome at nearly all clubs and events, had access to any and all DJs and promoters, and had the inside scoop on who was coming down to perform. Barely one year old, we were well known in the scene and had expanded our print run and pages.

The street promotion hustle opened even more doors. Thanks to Juan and Raul Sanchez, who was the hip hop buyer at Uncle Sam's and had also gotten into street teaming, we now had a direct line to some of the major label offices in New York and were sending copies and photos to marketing and promotion departments. It helped that our look and layout was more polished, and we had consistency as a bi-monthly publication with cover stories on artists who were hot at the time. We had sections such as 305 Live where we covered the clubs and shows, reviews of underground and commercial releases, poetry, graffiti, and knowledge of self. We were in our second act, the apex of our production of Miami's hip hop newspaper.

With so many shows taking place, seemingly by the week, we tried to cover them all: The Temple, this time at Club Amnesia (now Story) with Canibus, the Bob Marley festival at Bayfront Park, Club Boca every Monday night, the Winter Music Conference in March, raves, plus the usual clubs up and down Washington Avenue, we were everywhere and into all things. It's all a blur now, but looking back, the seeds for the beginning of the end were being planted. First, Heather Bee brought us the following obit:

I wanna start this report by dedicating it to the heads that represented up at Club Boca. Say farewell: "Cool World" has been deaded. This Monday night institution was the spot for true hip hop, with acts like Gang Starr, Black Moon, Common, Brand Nubian, and many more giving dope shows. Hip Hop Elements head Speedy Legs and Zulu Gremlin hosted the last event with another spectacular B-Boy/B-Girl showcase and DJ Slice on the 1's and 2's. Nightcrawler, B-Finesse, Stiff Rock, Troll, Chillski, MC Draztik and Junior on the congas set it off with techniques for that ass. Don't worry graf heads, there is gonna be time for y'all to shine at the 1999 B-Boy Masters Pro-Am; get ready for the event of the millennium kicking off the weekend of May 23rd. As for Cool World, Soul Kitchen Productions will be relocating to the Chili Pepper in Ft. Lauderdale. Now that the distance is shorter y'all don't have any excuse to miss out, na mean??

DMX (RIP)

Jermaine Dupri

Puff Daddy

Juvenile

Keep a look out for the "Temple of Hip Hop" hosted by DJ Stevie D and DJ Khaled. They will be having shows about twice a month on Monday nights. Then every Thursday will be college nights, so you know the steez. Back down in Dade, or should I say South Beach, Club Cream is back! Let's face it; they fell off for a minute. But all that drama don't even matter, cuz it has returned with DJ Kool G representing hip hop and reggae. Go check it out on Wednesday nights, and ladies don't forget you're in free before 12. See you there!

When you start to notice clubs getting shut down, relocating, off and on nights, resurrection attempts, you get a clear picture that the nightlife was in for a changing of the guard. Meanwhile, the rap industry had the city and even *The Cipher* in its clutches. By now we were all in with invites, VIP passes, and conference admissions. We were so large! It was nothing to roll up to Club Zen for Freaky Fridays as the Impact conference kicked off and skip all the heads in line, head straight to the door, and watch the velvet rope part as we flashed our press passes. Inside, Puff, J-Lo, and Bad Boy goons were holding down the VIP as we grooved to "It's All About the Benjamins baby (uh huh, yeah.)" Gone were the days of the Washingtons. Trying to document the festivities on film proved impossible, for as soon as our flash went off we were accosted by said goons and "politely" invited to put the cameras away.

Earlier that evening, we had jammed to De La Soul and Pharoahe Monch at the Sagamore Hotel. Thinking that hip hop culture would get its due within the rap industry, we were soon brought back to reality. We politicked our way to a Lil Kim album release party at Club Warsaw (now Señor Frog's) and had a nice chat. We were all the way down the rabbit hole now, and it would just keep getting deeper.

Of course, everyone knew she hardly wrote her rhymes, but her association with Big gave her a pass. It also helped that she had hot records every now and then. But the "female MC" segregation has always been ingrained in hip hop, with very few exceptions like Roxanne Shanté, MC Lyte, and Queen Latifah. Locally, we all rooted for Mother Superia, who filled us with pride when her "Most of All" video got played on Rap City. Here was a 305 representative with skills, not booty shaking, and about to blow up nationwide. Then…. nothing. Once again, the industry politics got in the way and that was that. Not even skills and Redman co-signs could take her to the next level. Perhaps it was the "female MC" stigma.

Now, back to the Impact Music Conference. Everybody from the hip hop industry is crashing in South Beach. Record labels are showcasing their artists at every possible spot available. Some people decided to forego the club rent-out price, and perform in the streets with a van convoy. Then there are others who hold their private party at the Fontainebleau Hilton in Miami Beach's upper class section. This is the case with Def Jam. DJing the event was the question mark man himself, DJ Clue? along with Funkmaster Flex and DJ Scratch spinning hot party hits that had the skin-tight packed ballroom jumping. Everyone in the crowd was feeling the vibe, including Guru, Channel Live, and Three-Six Mafia as they were tearing the club…well, the ballroom up. It would have been fine ending it at that, but what was to happen next, no one expected.

Suddenly, the lights go out and an anxious moment comes over the air as everyone waits to see what is about to occur. Then, on stage comes Slick Rick sitting on a throne with a crown on. The Ruler then goes on to perform "Mona Lisa," "Children's Story," and the new single "Street Talkin." Then, the lights go out again and a voice comes over the crowd: "It's been a long time since we've been together." All of a sudden, Doug E. Fresh pops on stage while everyone erupts into cheers. The duo of Slick Rick (with the gold) and Doug E. Fresh (beat boxing, oh yeah!) burst into performing the classics "Ladi Dadi" and "The Show." This is when the crowd was beyond euphoria—a once in a lifetime occurrence and no one expected it to happen. After they walk off, Ja Rule comes on stage to perform his new single "Holla, Holla" followed by another unexpected performer.

Jay-Z hops on stage, accompanied by Memphis Bleek and Beanie Seigel. The crowd explodes at the sight of Jigga while he breaks into performing "Nigga What, Nigga Who," "Can I Get a...," "It's Alright," "It's Murda," and various other platinum hits. Jay and Beanie also hit the crowd off with acapella freestyles which had everyone oohing and aahing. (They were real nasty. Ouch!) At the end of the night, Def Jam definitely blessed the people with a spectacular showcase of its artists. What a show and what a bargain. It was free!

I have to say this party was probably the climax of our club and *Cipher* experiences. First of all, we were in no way invited or even supposed to be there—it was a Def Jam showcase held at one of the most expensive hotels in town with tight security, no press, no guest list, strictly industry access. Nevertheless, we got wind of it and decided to roll to the Fontainebleau hoping to catch an interview or two. As we walked into the lobby, we saw Ja Rule exiting the elevator arm in arm with Gloria Velez, the top-heavy bleached blonde famous for her appearance in the "Big Pimpin" video. As expected, when we approached him for an interview of course he brushed us off. Who wants to talk to two backpackers when he's got a video model next to him? So we hang out and mill about waiting to see who we can corral when we notice the long line to get into the ballroom.

My first instinct is, "no way." Hulking security guards, Impact badges on display (which we had none), and a line that's not moving served as formidable obstacles. But I'm The Omen and this is *The Cipher,* and like Eminem, we just don't give a fuck! So Shareef and I head to the ballroom entrance and start the politics with the bouncer: Name dropping, free publicity, our people inside, any and everything short of greasing palms. (proud to say we never stooped to that level) But no dice.

So we backtracked, regrouped, and tried again with a different bouncer. To be frank, I think we overwhelmed him with our verbal calisthenics. You know those people that won't ever shut the fuck up? That was us. This time, the press angle worked, and we were let in past the velvet rope. Persistence does pay!

But it was the end. Nothing would be the same after that. That night, I saw the rap industry in its full expression and knew that in order to expand, we had to go corporate. Contracts, signed agreements, formal requests, rate sheets—all that back office behind the scenes stuff that I had no training or experience in. But after getting jacked by Black Gold, the Cristina episode, and the professional look we now sported, I had to try to work all the angles in order to prevent more drama. But the more I tried to fix it, the messier it got.

It would be great to say that our story had a happy ending like Wyclef's Carnival, but this is Miami and it just doesn't go down like that in the 305. Just like the clubs that shut down, record stores gave way to iTunes, Blockbuster bankrupted by Netflix. So too, *The Cipher* was put out to pasture. But unlike the physical structures that were destroyed by external forces, Miami's Hip Hop Newspaper was gutted and trashed from within. I, John Cordero aka Omen, played a big part in our own demise. Suicide, it was a suicide.

PART
:4:

EGO TRIPPIN'

In the first few months of 1999, we were making big moves externally, while internally we were imploding. Layout and design: beautiful. Articles and reviews: on point. Industry political connects: coming through with more and more access. But the staff and I were feeling the pressure.

Honest and I would stay up late nights, losing sleep over placements, space, ads, and deadlines, while I struggled with my day job, going through the motions just to pay bills and have fax access. Soon I was berating Honest for taking too long to design. What I thought was a simple task turned out to be anything but. In hindsight, it was like expecting him to knock out a long-form recap of the Impact conference in less than an hour. I took my time with my writing, editing, and re-editing. Why should I expect him to design and layout twenty four pages overnight?

Of course, he didn't appreciate that and it got us butting heads over the process. In the end, I learned that you can't rush greatness. So I took the L and tried to be a little more patient, while at the same time reassuring our sponsors that we were taking a little longer than expected because we were about to drop some hot shit.

Our back to school issue finally dropped at the end of August, and we had all angles covered: Miami representatives Da Alliance, Cue-45, and DJ Epps, B-Boy crew Ground Zeroh, and following up from the carnival, Wyclef Jean. The theme would be, once again, the B-Boy Masters Pro-Am. Speedy Legs was always down with the culture and with us so it was only right that we return the favor. No politics, just love for Miami Hip Hop:

As Hip Hop continues its climb to global dominance, its influence has extended to the far reaches of the world. Yet, amidst the glamour and platinum jewelry of your average rapper, there lurks a die-hard contingent of men and women who live, breathe, and sleep Hip Hop culture. While they are unjustly overlooked by the industry's need for the instant hit, these original schoolers maintain the honorable tradition of battling for the crown, showing skills, and earning respect.

The question that is most often asked, however, is: what happens when the spotlight no longer points in one's direction? Many of the legends we hear about today were once bonafide superstars. Did the Hard Knock Life and Bad Boy tours impress you? The Wild Style tour in 1982 took members of the Rock Steady Crew and NYC graf kings all over Europe and Japan. Mind you, Hip Hop didn't rule the charts back then and was often dismissed as a fad. Nevertheless, they made their names known far and wide. But the sands of time eroded their fame, leaving only scattered sediment of past glories.

Meanwhile, the new generation opted to let outside influence reinvent the wheel of history, setting in motion a roll of half-truths and assumptions. Books were written, movies made, and while some did manage to get the story straight, oftentimes they came up short. It became clear that only those who were actually there could pass on the legacy of this culture we call Hip Hop.

It was for this purpose among others that the B-Boy Masters Pro-Am was established. As the MC aspect of Hip Hop shot up to the stratosphere in terms of popularity, B-Boys and B-Girls were left on the sidelines and told by the media that their art form was "played out." The case became critical, especially in Miami, where a rich and profound Hip Hop history has been ignored and mostly forgotten, save for the originators. Consider Pro-Am co-founder Speedy Legs, whose tireless efforts to advance the cause of Hip Hop culture in the MIA are well documented. Although criticized by some, the record shows that he is one from a handful of original schoolers still active today and most importantly, shows no signs of slowing down.

Now in its third edition, Pro-Am has become the premiere B-Boy and B-Girl showdown. While the first was described as a "work in progress" by Speedy's partner Zulu Gremlin, and last year's a vast improvement but still soiled by a few blemishes, the 1999 version was nothing but four days of pure Hip Hop pleasure. The anticipation in the B-Boy community was running thick prior to May 20th, since a lot of beefs and feuds were going to get settled once and for all. Miami was the battleground from May 20th to the 23rd, and it would prove to be a landmark event.

B-Boy Masters Pro-Am for the new millennium

I didn't know it at the time, but this would be the last Pro-Am I would attend in a journalistic capacity. Speaking of innovation, one of the crews mentioned, Ground Zeroh, has been at the forefront of the B-Boy battle scene and continues to be in the vanguard today, passing the torch to a new generation:

In the B-Boy scene the crew is the glue that binds a group of individuals together in order to achieve a common goal: to dominate the dance floor. Take for example Miami's own Ground Zeroh Cru, who have been getting around the battle circuit for a while now. Members Bebe, Eckszooberant, Boo-Rok, Beta, Zemex, Legacy, and Neamz have all participated in numerous battles and competitions, with the outcome usually in their favor.

However, they do not assume the cocky attitude or front like they are the baddest. Simply staying tight and representing on the floor are their goals, and this work ethic has carried on through the decades as currently, they judge battles, choreograph video dance scenes, and release music. At the 1999 Pro-Am, I had the opportunity to speak to the president and co-founder Bebe, along with Zemex and star B-Girl Beta. They all shared insights into the B-Boy/B-Girl lifestyle and what it consists of. Regardless of what the Sprite commercials may tell you, it's not all about spinning on your head and getting props.

They went out of their way to pay respects to the legends and stressed the importance of having a good foundation. At the same time, they were confident enough to know that they had next and were itching to blow, which they did. More battles, more wins, and more props. What stuck out to me was the maturity level of these (at the time) high school kids. If only the up and coming generation in the 305 had the same mentality, but you know how that goes...

They also brought up valid criticisms of the commercial scene, and I was right there with them. But when it came to clubbing, I wasn't only a client, I was the VIP president. Along with Club Cream, another club and promotion entity showed us much love. Of course, it was all about the polys. Steady coverage guaranteed continued access, and for much of 1999 the one place you wanted to be every Friday night was Club Zen's "Freaky Fridays" put on by Nightbreederz Entertainment with DJ Epps on the 1's and 2's. Now boarded up, this legendary spot saw some truly over-the-top shenanigans as partygoers filled the venue to capacity every Friday night.

The beach is notorious for its residential instability (the average time a restaurant, store, or club stays around is about four months.) But despite these odds, Nightbreederz Entertainment maintained the crowds for three years, which is pretty impressive. What is the secret, you may ask? DJ Epps, the man responsible for the beats, simply replies, "Holdin' down the crowd, that's what it's about." Big Stats, another Nightbreederz soldier, gives *The Cipher* a second key ingredient (and probably the most important one) in the success of the freakiest spot on the beach: "Keep the

Aaliyah (RIP) performing
in Miami—1999

Heather Lawrence

Jam Master Jay (RIP) of Run-DMC
performing at The Cameo—
Miami 1999

Heather Lawrence

crowd coming? We got a lot of ladies, that's how! Everyone comes to see the ladies. We have them free before 1 AM; they show up looking freaky and crazy. So in turn, the fellas come chasing. It's all about treating the ladies right."

But for all you new jack promoters thinking that a recipe like the above can be easily replicated, think again. DJ Epps is the man who controls the crowd through rhythmic commands, from "stop, drop, shut 'em down" to "heads high, kill 'em wid it now," this Haitian brother has introduced a whole new generation to the colloquial greeting "Sak Pasé." "People always want to know, what is Sak Pasé? And I wanna represent right. It basically means 'what's going on?' 'What's up,' 'what the deally, yo' [in Kreyol] and it's all peace when the crowd responds," he states.

But he wants it known: he's extending this greeting to all the Hip Hop masses regardless of national origin. "[It's for] all Cubans, Colombians, Dominicans, Jamaicans, Trinis, white, Black, Chinese, it don't matter." When asked about the growth of Hip Hop on a national and local scale, DJ Epps responds, "I'm amazed at how far we've come, but I know Hip Hop is taking over everything. Pretty soon, countries are gonna be put aside, armies are gonna be with us, and there's gonna be Hip Hop everywhere! The world is gonna be locked down, because all we want is Hip Hop."

Perhaps Epps' Hip Hop New World Order might be a little ambitious, but he does have very practical advice for all Hip Hop hopefuls striving to be successful in any aspect of the entertainment industry: "Control your own shit! Me, I control my shit with my crew. They got my back, I got theirs, and this is how we living. If you do your business right, there's no reason why you can't have your big pile of money. Just do for self, and if you decide to work for others, make sure everything's straight, and you can't go wrong."

"Freaky Fridays" has already become the standard response to the question "where the party at?" and Epps is more than happy to oblige all the freaks lusting for their fix. From the days of the Sugar Shack till now, this young and enterprising Killian High graduate will continue to bring the good times and command the crowds. So next time you hear the booming voice from the DJ booth asking "Sak Pasé?" you know it's all about that "Nap Boulé!" and the party goes on...

Nightbreederz kept it on lock for the rest of the year and into the new millennium until the normal nightclub fate finally claimed it. DJ Epps went on to host music conferences, affiliate himself with the Shadyville and G-Unit DJs, and can now be heard Friday nights on Vibe 92.7 FM in Miami and on Sirius XM, a true testament to the hustler spirit. Speaking of hustlers, we weren't ready for what we discovered one night at the Publix parking lot in Kendall's Town & Country strip mall.

Shareef had tapped into the new talent through the scene grapevine, and told me about this new cat (better yet, canine) that was coming up and spitting hard shit. His government name was Armando Perez, but he went by Pitbull. He was on the verge of

Cam'Ron—Miami 1999

signing to Luke Records, but still found time to meet up with us in Kendall and spit some rhymes along with passing us his demo tape.

Now, I had heard all kinds of local rappers. I've always been into lyrics and could count on one hand the number of Miami rappers that I rated highly in that department. Maybe this was the reason no one ever got put on? Guru said, "It's mostly the voice." KRS-One said, "They can't write a song, so their careers don't last long." I agree with both of them. Truth is, on top of talent and ability, the undefinable trait needed to make it in show business is charisma. Entertainers live and die by it. It can't be taught, can't be practiced.

I write this as I remember a young, hungry, and unknown Pitbull rhyming for us in the Town & Country parking lot. When he was done, Shareef and I looked at each other like, "Yo!" We had no idea he would go on to become "Mr. Worldwide," and of course he wasn't doing Spanglish party verses back then, but we could tell that his charisma and stage presence were leaps and bounds above what we had heard up to then. Chris wrote up the review of his first single:

> Miami moneymakers now have an official anthem, courtesy of one of the illest up-and-coming MCs to ever spring from down south. "Fuck you, Pay me" is the single from Miami native Pitbull, whose skills demonstrate that there is still a lot of untapped star potential in the M.I.A. With a dark beat laced with creative futuristic layering, this is a single destined to be bumped in your ride. Beats are provided by Crystal Entertainment and rhymes by Pit, whose intense lyrical visuals will give you flashbacks to the violent get-money tactics of Scarface: "Nigga fuck you, pay me/trigga buck you, spray me/nah dawg/I see it like this: M.I.A.M.I/all about that down south M.O.N.E.Y/to the niggas pullin triggas for figures/on the block where the sluts at/yo drop my drop/oh my bad bitch, this my block/betta buck down when I cock back." The song's entrancing stick 'em up hook will have all the thugs suffering from the nod factor as this is a definite Miami essential for your collection.

It's ironic that we found Pitbull as we were on the verge of disintegrating. Another up and coming soon-to-be star who was just beginning to get his name out was Rick Ross. We never met him,

Roni Size Reprazent—in-store event
at Spec's Music (RIP)
South Beach 1999

but his first forays as a local artist on Slip-n-Slide Records (home to Miami legends Trick Daddy and Trina) were just being released.

The late nights, stress, drama, and self-inflicted wounds had taken their toll. While Pitbull and Rick Ross went on to great success, we were on our next-to-last issue. 1999 was about to end, Y2K was gonna cause havoc, and *The Cipher* had one foot in the grave. Heather wasn't going out without a fight though. Loyal and committed to the very end, she politicked and hustled non-stop in a bid to expand our coverage and attempt to get more advertisers.

Meanwhile, I was deep into the rave scene, specifically drum'n'bass, breaks, and downtempo. Andy C, Ed Rush & Optical, Goldie, Shy FX, Ram Trilogy, Metalheadz, J-Majik, Dillinja, DJ Hype, Reprazent, DJ Icey, DJ Baby Anne, Rabbit In The Moon, The Prodigy, Chemical Brothers, Talvin Singh, DJ Shadow, Massive Attack, Portishead, Everything But The Girl, DJ Spooky, Aphex Twin, Air, Thievery Corporation, 4 Hero, DJ Krush, Asian Dub Foundation, pretty much any and everything coming out of a synthesizer and sampler. As hip hop was jigged out and corporatized to the max, I expanded my sonics to fresh new beats, hold the rhymes and add female vocals. 160 BPM jungle vibes to get hyped, funky Florida breaks, and chilled out downtempo for the comedown after the party was what I was all about.

From its humble beginnings at South Beach clubs, The Edge in Ft. Lauderdale, Studio 183 in Miami Gardens, and abandoned warehouses off Krome Avenue, the South Florida rave scene had grown so large that five thousand plus in attendance at every event was the norm. Promoters Russell Faibisch and Alex Omes banded together and founded the Ultra Music Festival, whose very first party was held on March 13th, 1999 at the beach's Collins Park (literally... as in on the sand) off 23rd and Collins, where hippie drum circles had been taking place for years.

I arrived that afternoon to find thumping beats behind a wraparound fence enclosure, and it was laughably easy to sneak underneath it and PLUR my ass off to DJ Baby Anne, Paul van Dyk, and headliners Rabbit in the Moon, whose infamous live show had to be seen to be believed. From then on I was a faithful UMF devotee, attending the next four years at the beach and then at Bayfront Park, never having paid the outrageous ticket prices. I was a true blue gatecrasher!

Meanwhile, as proof of how far *The Cipher* had come, Columbia Records sent us a stack of promo photos, the Kool Keith "Black Elvis/Lost in Space" album advance, press kit, and PR rep contact info to arrange an interview. Calling up the office in NYC, I couldn't help but reminisce on cutting and pasting, driving all over town for an interview, and transcribing word for word. Now, major labels had us on their distribution list and Honest laid everything out on Photoshop.

Phife, Guru, and Kool Keith. Three very different MCs who I grew up listening to, and managed to interview under very different circumstances: a somber and downcast Phife post-ATCQ breakup backstage at Studio 183, an amped and upset Guru at Club Boca, and a Kool Keith who was just going through the major label motions over the phone. Those three, plus the Lyricist Lounge show at Cameo with De La Soul, the Temple with Fat Joe and Big Pun, and the Dungeon Family Super Bowl weekend showcase also at Cameo were the highlights of my *Cipher* run. Of course, who can forget the "impossible to get in" Def Jam spectacle at the Fontainebleau and the RSC anniversary weekend in NYC. Seeing those legends perform live, some of whom are no longer with us, made all the drama worth it. There was also my first time seeing the Roots crew live, over Halloween weekend '99:

So the kids drive up to Boca Raton, about an hour from Miami, just to trick or treat at Florida Atlantic University. Hearing about the bountiful aural candy to be enjoyed at this institution of higher partying made The Cipher children anxious to run about and fill their bags. Knocking doors at an open-air venue? Gotta keep it surreal.

Ghouls and goblins were few and far between, as the Hip Hop masses converged with the threat of rainout looming ominously above our heads. However, the clouds parted and lo and behold! The legendary 5th Dynasty takes the stage decked out in monk robes. Instead of raisins and stale gum, Black Thought dipped into his bag and gave lyrical treats for the kiddies in the form of freestyles and Roots classics such as "Silent Treatment," "100% Dundee," and "Adrenaline." But it was the rock version of "You Got Me" that had heads wilding out in the neighborhood.

Cut to a ?uestlove drum solo, Kamaal's Klangskwad hootin' and hollerin', and Hub's bass mechanics, all followed by Scratch's verbal turntablism. No Roots show would be complete without the Hip Hop history lesson aptly dubbed

"Hip Hop 101." Easily violating curfew by staying through a 2 and ½ hour set, youngsters went home with a severe case of cavities from all the sweets provided by the Okayplayers, making "Teeth Fall Apart" a more fitting name for an LP.

?uestlove later mentioned how playing these college shows paved the way for the mega-payday the Roots are now enjoying: "Corporate…This is the quickest way to make a fast buck. These gigs didn't kick in [until] late in our career because yesterday's college student who was mind-blown in '96 is now organizing the ATT trip in Nawlins and has a budget for the Roots…college is the seed that will sprout into your garden in the future. Simply put, all these commercials and Nike deals and movie scoring and whatever, 'How the hell did he get that?' was because I played the *shit* outta colleges. And if you are nice to them, *they remember,* so when they graduate and get put on? *You are the first person they come gunning for.* All the college gigs we did are *so* paying off right now."

Speaking of paying off, the convention hustle kept on. First, the Mixshow Power Summit, held from September 29th to October 3rd, 1999, which was aimed at radio and club jocks and was organized to give them shine. The parties and shows were a godsend, as acts like De La Soul and Pharoahe Monch performed their hits in the South Beach rap industry playground. By the end of '99, I was completely burned out from the nightlife grind, so new *Cipher* writer Ozzie Alfonso took the reins of the MPS as we chose to cover one label showcase a night.

Kool G Rap at Crazy Goods store—Miami 1999

Politickin' with RZA at the
How Can I Be Down?
conference

Women in business pan

Def Jam President Kevin Liles
shares a laugh

Funkmaster Flex gets seriou

Heather Lawrence

Heather Lawrence

I found Ozzie a welcome relief for my writing duties. I was *done*. I had next to no interest in reviews, shows, interviews, nothing at all. The grind was unbearable. Fighting and arguing with Honest had us at each other's throats almost daily. He too had quit and we were forced to scramble to find another designer for our last issue. We didn't know it was to be our last: there was no official announcement, no goodbye to the readers.

On that note, what could be a more fitting piece to run in *The Cipher*'s very last issue than a wrap-up of my nemesis, my bête noire, my perpetual antagonist: the How Can I Be Down? conference. To start, I hated, *hated*, that name. Bro, I'm *already* down! I've been down with hip hop since my older cousin took me to see Beat Street in 1983. My mom bought me bootlegs of LL Cool J's "Bigger And Deffer" and Run-DMC's "Raising Hell" at a flea market. Another cousin bought me NWA's "Straight Outta Compton" because it had the parental advisory sticker. In 1989 when I came to the U.S, it was all a dream: I used to read *Word Up!* magazine…and *Fresh!* and *Right On!*

I never went to the original HCIBD?, which ran from 1993 to 1996 in South Beach. Hoodstock's "You'z Already Down" tagline was way more attractive to me. But in 1999, with DJ Raw locked up and HCBID? being allowed to return after the Montego Bay editions saw a dramatic dip in attendance, a much quieter edition (read: no shots fired) prevailed. Heather and I politicked our way in and this is how we experienced it:

> "It's the infamous, back in the house once again…" Mobb Deep's lyrics took on additional meaning when the much maligned How Can I Be Down? music conference

touched down in Miami Beach on October 9th and 10th, 1999. Having established itself as the premier rap industry convention as well as party capital, HCIBD? ran into city council roadblocks and was forced to relocate to Jamaica in 1997.

Banned from South Beach, this year's edition was centered in neighboring North Bay Village. Where once there were all-night parties complete with shootings and partiers galore, attendees would witness a much subdued and calmer atmosphere this time around. Def Jam president Kevin Liles, Funkmaster Flex, and The RZA were some of the panelists, and the discussions proved to be a learning experience for the multitude of up-and-coming rappers in attendance. Following is a short summary of each panel as well as highlights showing how you too can get paid in the new millennium.

"Show Me The Money: Publishing, Royalties, and Copyright Administration"

This informative panel sought to describe one of the hidden aspects of the music business while at the same time dispelling the myths associated with it. Although by now it is common knowledge that artists on average make a dollar per record sold, most people don't know that publishing is where the majority of the money is made. Panelists advised artists and writers to never sign over their publishing rights to a label, and to always register with performing rights organizations such as BMI or ASCAP to ensure the proper payment of royalties. These are steps that should be followed before releasing a record, with no exceptions.

"Having More Power: Making More Money (My Own Label)"

It was fitting that HCIBD? featured an independent label panel, given the explosion of small-budget labels within the last few years. Speaking about the process involved in pushing one's own record were Dame Grease from Vacant Lot Productions and The RZA, who both agreed that getting radio play is a difficult task in the era of payola (yes, it does exist) and that independent artists should look for auxiliary markets. RZA also stressed the need to be clean-cut when dealing with corporate America, while maintaining communication with peers. Both also stressed dedication to the product and hustling skills. RZA summed it up: "If you got enough money to last, you will. It's not overnight success."

"Entertainment's Guerilla Warfare: (Mixshow DJs, Underground Radio, Compilations, Mixtapes, and Street Teams)"

Inquiring minds want to know: did Funkmaster Flex ever take a payoff from a label to play a record? That seemed to be the underlying theme at this panel, judging by the questions from the audience. Flex relayed a story of having pocketed $200 from a small label in the early 90's,

Welcome to Ultra!

DJ Rap (R) at Ultra Music Festival—Miami 2000

only to have the caper uncovered. He warned DJs not to take the easy money unless they are ready for their reps to be ruined. Panelist Big Kap added: "Self-promotion is the best promotion." Since the usual practice is to pay a firm to promote the product, it's best to keep everything in-house and do all promoting from within. Flex also stated, "If the person doesn't believe in what they're pushing, it means nothing."

Also discussed were politics (The Cipher's favorite), in which Def Jam president Kevin Liles said that one must work hard to develop relationships, since success in the industry is based on good relationships. Once again Flex dropped the following jewel: "For everyone that makes it, a thousand don't."

"The Next Wave (New Media Technologies & Strategies)"

Acknowledging the power of the Internet, this panel sought to enlighten the few who aren't yet online to take advantage of the vast cyber-audience. Manager Amelia Moore related the case of her clients, The Mountain Brothers, who were able to utilize the net to expand their fan base at minimal cost—employing websites, email lists, chats, and banners as marketing tools. However, she cautioned artists not to give up their domain names, which companies such as Sony have been incorporating as clauses in contracts. Panelists also mentioned the ease of learning HTML (the computer

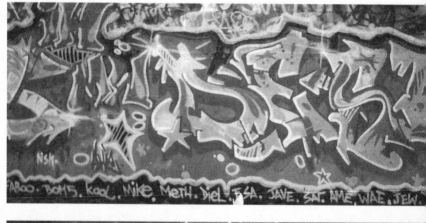

ABOO. BOM5. KOOL. MIKE. METH. DIEL. ESA. JAVE. SAT. AME. WAE. JEW.

language used to create web pages) and the need to master it, as it is a powerful marketing tool.

"The Globalization of Hip Hop (International and Emerging Markets)"

One of the most important things we as Americans often forget is what else is out there in the world. There are things to remember when marketing your artist, company, label, or productions. One must never forget, there is more to the world than just the U.S.A. Your average person would rather not be bothered with all the hassles involved in getting the product overseas. A strong distribution firm is needed.

For instance, the distribution panel featured Figure IV Entertainment. With this firm, one doesn't have to worry about the complications of distributing products abroad. Anyone could be doing one million in sales in the U.S. and completely sleep on the other two million in France, Germany, or Italy. We all know promotion is the key to success, so don't let frustration and the lack of planning hold you back.

Here are some ideas that were discussed over the panel before getting involved with a distribution company: first, do your homework on them and make sure your product is going to where it needs to be. Next, take the opportunity within yourself and the company. Finally, get your product out there and make it happen.

Ladies, ladies, ladies…when entering this wonderful world, the so-called "entertainment business" we often come across minor setbacks. In this particular situation, I am referring to men. We as women in the business are often pushed back, set aside, and almost completely overlooked. Now, these incidents often happen when you're getting observed as a piece of easy meat.

While listening and relating to certain similar incidents from the panel, things all started to make sense. Unfortunately, we have no control over an industry dominated by men. However, we are slowly and surely coming up as women. Yes, there are women already, like the ones on the panel and many more who are doing their thing, and keep doing it even stronger than men.

This is not a debate between men and women; it's more or less a reality check. The panelists stressed the need to stay in control of the situation, know what's going on, stay professional, and believe in your product. Don't ever give up on what you want and truly believe in. With the new millennium approaching us, you may be the next to make that move and succeed in what you have always believed in."

Needless to say, the professional demeanor and congenial atmosphere stood in sharp contrast to prior HCIBD?, owing largely in fact to it being formally banned from Miami Beach city limits. Over the years, it would die out as Peter Thomas moved on to other business ventures and more recently, Love and Hip Hop.

As for *The Cipher*, Heather was determined to fight on, but I was finished. She was soon to move to Washington DC and link up with a Webmaster there, but obviously it wasn't the same.

Now, all good things must come to an end. The MPS would be the last "party in the VIP with rappers" conference I would attend, as I had moved on to Ultra and the WMC, which would become my new home in the 2G. But for my grand closing, I politicked my way into a corporate marketing conference at the Bal Harbour Sheraton. I'll never forget rolling to one of the most exclusive zip codes in Miami in my beat-up Honda, with the muffler on the verge of falling off, and handing my keys to the valet as I exited.

Yes, I was that "fake it 'til you make it" guy. I was hyped because I had connected with Tina Imm of platform.net, which was the go-to for the nascent streetwear scene. My dreams of baggin' Triple 5 Soul and the major corporations present at the conference for advertising in *The Cipher* were crushed soon after, but for a couple of days I was in the room with the behind the scenes movers and shakers all trying to market to the Hip Hop audience.

"Seize your share of the exploding youth market." These were the calling words that lured corporations such as Ford, NBA, HBO, Pepsi, and Nike, judging by major marketing executives attending the "Welcome to the Hip Hop Generation" conference held in Miami Beach on November 17-18th, 1999. Made possible thanks to the Strategic Research Institute, a top marketing research firm, the two-day presentation also featured established Hip Hop companies Enyce, RP 55, platform.net, and Bad Boy Entertainment. Devoid of the usual distractions that often accompany these sorts of gatherings, the focus was strictly business oriented. The fact that it took place during a workweek and was closed to the public made it more even conducive to a learning and networking environment.

The overall theme was one of building an image that the consumer (you) can identify with. Wanda Austin-Wingood, Urban and Ethnic Marketing Manager at Pepsi, spoke about the concept of brand affinity. In her words, "Brand affinity is a by-product of passion, preference, and intensity about a brand." She also mentioned how subsidiary Mountain Dew's sales and overall image among the "18 to 24 urban demo[graphic]" increased by approximately 30% due to the endorsement of Busta Rhymes. Her advice to other companies: "Identify, talk, and listen to your target." Following her presentation, HBO's Senior Manager of Brand Promotions, Sherrie Curette, presented a case study of Heat center Alonzo Mourning's annual Zo's Summer Groove charity event. Once again the power of the celebrity spokesman was manifested as HBO's title sponsorship resulted in a 192% increase in HBO upgrades for the South Florida market.

Another marketing tool employed by companies is "Urban Branding." Courtney Sloane, President and Creative Director of the NYC-based Alternative Design firm, mentioned that the "Hip Hop demo has a world of imagination" and that in order to reach this audience, companies should know their client and consumer by gathering information and understanding the culture and language. AD's credentials include designing the Hip Hop Exhibit at the Rock

DJ Snowhite

Goodie Mob—Miami 1999

Clockwise L-R: DJ Slice, DJ Snowhite, DJ Craze, DJ Infamous, and DJ NV—Miami 1999

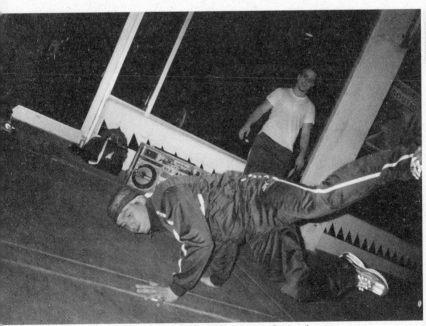

Louie of StreetMasters crew with some floorwork

& Roll Hall of Fame in Cleveland, as well as marketing campaigns for BET, Vibe, Bad Boy, and more.

From a marketing standpoint, the highlight of the conference was the Ford Focus campaign. Brand Manager Julie Roehm explained step-by-step the process of selling a new car to an estimated one hundred million strong audience (Echo boomers and Generation X). With data collected from research, Ford has developed websites and employed hip hop street teams to sell cars to a generation that looks upon Ford as a traditional car marker. A key point made was the way they are looking to concentrate on the five areas that influence consumers: music, fashion, sports, technology, and entertainment. It seems they have done their homework in marketing to the hip hop generation, utilizing slick ads and a custom-made CD-ROM that will help buyers and even tell you when your car needs an oil change.

No marketing conference would be complete without mention of the fastest-growing audience in America: so-called Latinos. Jorge Cano-Moreno, publisher of *Urban Latino* magazine, emphasized the need for companies to recognize this diverse market and specifically pointed out that what appeals to a Puerto Rican in New York will not necessarily resonate with a Mexican in Texas. Also pointing out the need for diversity was Tina Imm of platform.net, who advised companies that a web presence is not enough in today's marketplace.

The conference ended with The Source Entertainment's Mike Elliott detailing the process for The Source Awards. With only twelve weeks of working time, all departments (circulation, editorial,

Chillski of Deadly Venoms crew- B-Boy Masters Pro-Am—Miami 1999

Deadly Venoms crew—Miami 1999

advertising, and production) produced the 4th highest rated special in UPN history. Citing the statistics of 1998 (Rap sold 81 million albums, up 31%, hip hop related fashion generated approximately one billion dollars in revenue, Lauryn Hill sold an estimated twenty-one million records worldwide, Jay-Z set a Billboard record by spending five straight weeks at number one, DMX outsold Garth Brooks and also set a record by having two platinum albums debut at number one in the same year), and *The Source* staff managed to sell prime-time thirty second spots at seventy-five thousand dollars, resulting in a sell-out of ad space. UPN is now looking forward to next year's awards.

What do all these figures and strategies mean to the average hip hop consumer? In my opinion, it is evident that Corporate Americas' foray into hip hop was inevitable. Numbers never lie, and when Jay-Z sells five million records, CEOs and marketing departments take notice. The fact that the Hip Hop buying audience is seventy percent white might also be a validating point. As *The Source*'s Peter Ferraro put it, "The kid listening to Limp Bizkit really wants to be Jay-Z anyway."

You can only imagine what size my head was when I rolled out of there at the end of the conference. These companies have millions of dollars to spend on advertising! Surely a few thousand here and there will mean nothing for them. Finally we can publish in color! Put up a proper website! Expand circulation! Sell, sell, sell! I personally spoke and traded cards with nearly everyone—these were heads of marketing departments, not lackeys. The promised land was right around the corner!

Unfortunately, it was not to be. Aside from Tina, who was down with putting our content on platform.net, everyone else gave me the brush off. Why would they do business with a local b&w newspaper when Dave Mays of *The Source* was there and already had them all under contract? Forget the fact that I and plenty of others had stopped reading The Sauce a long time ago as its editorial content became a press release service for Benzino, and that Napster was just around the corner waiting to blow their whole business model to shit.

Frustrated and angry, I bowed out, this time for good. The dream had come to an end. Too many fights, stress over publishing deadlines, printing costs, and the lack of financial resources soured my plans. All of it combined became too much to bear so I resigned from *The Cipher* and quit the "rap industry." I turned down the Jay-Z, turned up the U.N.K.L.E, and walked. My personal life was a disaster: broke, car falling apart, couch surfing, college drop-out, single, credit card debt, the whole enchilada. I was close to Shareef and Honest, but burnt out and stressed to the max, my emotional outbursts took a toll on my friendships.

It was particularly brutal between Honest and I since I was crashing at his crib and after one too many fights, I got kicked out and had to couch surf for a couple of months. Eventually, I found a job at an export company in Doral and saved enough to get an efficiency in the Gables. I had to start from zero *again*, but I made it. Almost 20 years later, both of us now grown men, Honest (now living in Amsterdam after making a name for himself in the art world) and I linked up at the 2017 Art Basel and we had a great time rocking out at the Wu-Tang reunion show… after I apologized for my immature behavior.

At the time *The Cipher* ended, I had a fallout with a girl I was seeing. After relaying the story of how I did her dirty to Shareef, he dropped all contact with me. It would remain that way until we talked it out and shook hands several years later. But to show and prove how life always comes full circle like a cipher, I now sublet a condo from him in downtown Miami. Word up.

Method Man got himself a shorty—Miami 1998

EPILOGUE

Now in 2022, what's become of the Miami Hip Hop scene? DJ Craze is a family man and record label owner (Slow Roast Records) that has and continues to spin all over the world. DJ Khaled is a major motivational meme and catchphrase-generating celebrity with platinum hits and six million Snapchat followers. Pitbull hosts New Year's Eve concerts on a major TV network. Ground Zero Crew tours and promotes B-Boy battles. Coop D Vill splits his time spinning records in Hawaii and the Bay Area. DJ Epps is on the radio nightly on Vibe 92.7 FM in Miami and on "Rock The Bells" on SiriusXM.

DJ Infamous produces for Lil Wayne, Yo Gotti, Drake, and others and wins Grammys. Crook and Crome paint legal productions and work as graphic designers and illustrators. DJ EFN is at the top of the download charts with the "Drink Champs" podcast, co-hosted with Noreaga. Edecsta exhibits his work in art galleries. Wynwood is now a world-famous tourist art destination covered in graffiti with some of the most expensive real estate in Miami. DJ Uncle Al, Mic Rippa, Rol-Up from Flava Station, and Oil/FS are resting in peace.

Ultra is bigger and bigger every year: tickets start at $350. South Beach is a tourist-trap shell of its former hedonistic party self: all the clubs mentioned in this book are extinct but bottle service VIP clubs such as Liv and Story keep the nightlife and dollars flowing while most locals party in Brickell and Wynwood now. DJ Raw has been released from prison and lives a quiet family life in Broward as an entrepreneur. The Universal Zulu Nation-Miami Chapter has been revived and educates the new generation. Crazy

Hood Productions remains in effect, and has recently released the fifth "Coming Home" documentary, set in Colombia.

Honest Benevolent is a sculptor and fine artist who travels the world. After working at Slip-n-Slide Records and managing Plies, Shareef is now an international entrepreneur based overseas. Heather Bee has a family with two beautiful sons and is getting that real estate money. The legacy we were a part of and the hip hop lifestyle we lived and championed has either evolved into nostalgia, inability to get into the new generation's output, and/or questions of aging into a youth-driven culture. Just as Miami has changed dramatically since I arrived 27 years ago, so has hip hop. The biggest rap star at the moment is a Canadian "singing nigga" who bodies so-called tough guys from Philly (Beanie Sigel wept). MacBooks and Serato have replaced crates and vinyl. Former graffiti outlaws sell thousand-dollar pieces at Art Basel.

The generation before mine argued over who was the best MC: Rakim, Kane, or KRS-One. Mine argued over Biggie, Jay-Z, or Nas (for the record, it's God's Son). The present generation argues over Drake, J. Cole, or Kendrick Lamar. In fifteen years the next generation will argue over another triumvirate. Change is inevitable, progress undeniable. The penits, clubs, stores, vinyl, and, in some cases, the people may be physically gone, but the essence of creating and dropping heat remains in the 305, the M.I.A., the Magic City, the Rokk Bottom of the map.

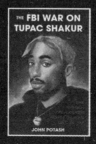